THE SERMON AS GOD'S WORD

•

Theologies for Preaching

Robert W. Duke

ABINGDON PREACHER'S LIBRARY

William D. Thompson, Editor

ABINGDON
Nashville

The Sermon as God's Word: Theologies for Preaching

Copyright © 1980 by Abingdon

Library of Congress Cataloging in Publication Data

DUKE, ROBERT W.
   The sermon as God's word.
   (Abingdon preacher's library)
   Bibliography: p.
   Includes index.
   1. Preaching—History—20th century.
   2. Theology, Doctrinal—History—20th century. I. Title.
   BV4207.D84   230'.044   80-18094

ISBN 0-687-37520-7

Scripture quotations are from the Revised Standard Version
of the Bible, copyrighted © 1946, 1952, © 1971, 1973.

MANUFACTURED BY THE PARTHENON PRESS AT
NASHVILLE, TENNESSEE, UNITED STATES OF AMERICA

THE SERMON AS GOD'S WORD

Abingdon Preacher's Library

**To my wife
ELSBETH**

CONTENTS

EDITOR'S FOREWORD

Preaching has captured the attention of increasingly large segments of the American public. Lay parish committees seeking pastoral leadership consistently rank preaching as the most desirable pastoral skill. Seminary courses and clergy conferences on preaching attract participants in larger numbers than ever. Millions of viewers watch television preachers every week.

What is *good* preaching? is the question of both those who hear it and those who do it. Hearers answer that question instinctively, tuning in the preacher who meets their needs, whether in the pulpit of the neighborhood church or on a broadcast. Preachers need to answer more intentionally.

Time was that a good thick book on preaching would do it, or a miscellaneous smattering of thin ones. The time now seems ripe for a different kind of resource—a carefully conceived, tightly edited series of books whose scope covers the homiletical spectrum and whose individual volumes reveal the latest and best thinking about each specialty within the field of preaching. The volumes in the Abingdon Preacher's Library enable the preacher to understand preaching in its historical setting; to examine its biblical and theological underpinnings; to explore its spiritual, relational, and liturgical dimensions; and to develop insights into its craftsmanship.

Designed primarily for use in the seminary classroom, this series will also serve the practicing preacher whose background in homiletics is spotty or out-of-date, or whose preaching needs strengthening in some specific area.

William D. Thompson
Eastern Baptist Theological Seminary
Philadelphia, Pennsylvania

I. INTRODUCTION

This book examines a variety of theologies in order to show how the preacher's choice and development of a text is shaped by assumptions of which he or she may not consciously be aware. I am certain we all have noticed how differently a number of preachers may use the same text. We often wonder how they got those sermons out of *that* text! Helmut Thielicke, for example, a German Lutheran pastor, and Harry Emerson Fosdick, an American Baptist pastor, both have written and published famous sermons on the parable of the prodigal son. When one reads with care, it becomes clear that the dominant motif of Thielicke's sermon is the role of the waiting father. The main theme of Fosdick's sermon, on the other hand, is the need and ability of the prodigal son to rise up out of his despair and return home. The first sermon stresses the active, seeking role of the father, while the second places the main accent upon the positive role of the son.

It is true, of course, that sermons about this parable vary as to emphasis and theme, as any brief study of the history of preaching would quickly show. It also may be true that both Thielicke and Fosdick delivered sermons, yet unpublished, which develop other elements of the same story. Nevertheless, I believe a good case can be made for claiming that both preachers tended to construct sermons with themes that remain more or less constant. This constancy occurs because each had fairly fixed theological presuppositions about God, about God's revelation to us in Jesus Christ, and about Christ's influence in shaping our lives. Both made assumptions about human nature growing out of such reflections, in addition to being shaped in their theological understanding by the cultures in which they lived.

I intend to show how such assumptions affect the sermons of several preachers who, I believe, influence a broad spectrum of preaching today. Their themes are the roots from which we already may, consciously or not, be fed. Indeed, as the arguments are developed, the reader should carry on a conversation with him- or herself, and with the preachers involved, in order to become more thoroughly aware of his or her own belief-system.

It is essential to know how to exegete texts and how to construct sermons based upon them. A good deal of time is properly devoted to this essential procedure in basic courses in preaching. What needs further examination is the theological process going on in the preachers who are working at this task. What assumptions do we hold concerning Jesus Christ? What picture do we have of his ministry, death, and resurrection? We rightly argue that our sermons are to meet the needs of people from the perspective of the gospel; but how do we envision these people, and what is the good news in our age for them? All these reflections, half-formed or unknown, are theological concerns of which we need to be aware, because we bring them to the text when we study it and preach from it.

This book's approach is to study *sermons*, not theological writings, since I believe it is in the crucible of the Sunday sermon that the church's theology is most decisively formed. I have chosen the five major theological traditions of the twentieth century that seem to me to have been most influential in shaping theology in today's pulpits. Some traditions seem to come alive most readily through the study of the work of one preacher—Karl Barth, Paul Tillich, or Albert Cleage; others—namely liberalism and fundamentalism—require a survey of many preachers. Choosing representative preachers in these categories is difficult if not impossible, but I have tried to present each position fairly. If a theological position is more clear at one of its extremes—for instance, in the preaching of Albert Cleage—I have used his work rather than that of a preacher at the center of that movement.

I have omitted the more recent theological trends—process, relational, charismatic, feminist, developmental, the theology of hope, and the emerging evangelical theology—not because they are unimportant, but because they are, at this writing, still in the process of forming, maturing, or even dying. Nor is there, in most instances, a significant body of sermonic literature upon which to draw. And I have left to another time or another writer the systematic consideration of the "eclectic" theology—this is the only label one can use for what happens in many American pulpits on a given Sunday. Although it may be a kind of eclectic theology that really embodies what this book is all about: the shaping of one's own theology of preaching, while drawing upon a rich sermonic-theological heritage.

In shaping that personal preaching theology, it seems to me that increasingly, we need to get in touch with ourselves and to take our own feelings, conceptions, and assumptions with utmost seriousness. It is my hope that this book will contribute to an enrichment of our own self-understanding and widen our horizons concerning the subject matter of sermons and the way they take the forms they do. To preach effectively, we must struggle with the task of dealing not only with the objective material in the text, but also with our subjective attitudes and belief-systems as well. Sermons proclaim the gospel, but they proclaim "my" gospel as well.

I. NEO-ORTHODOXY: KARL BARTH

We can come to God only through God himself.
                                        Karl Barth

It seems appropriate to begin with an examination and evaluation of Karl Barth's preaching. Perhaps no other preacher/theologian in this century has devoted more thought and writing to preaching, not only in the form of published sermons, but in theological treatises as well. The first two volumes of his *Church Dogmatics* are devoted to what many have called a neo-orthodox theology of preaching, and the remainder deal with the rich sermonic mine afforded by the quality of theological reflection. In reading *Church Dogmatics*, one may be overwhelmed by the intricate argument and reasoned development and might ask if sermons really do rest on such a massive base? Is this, one is tempted to wonder, the work of a reclusive theologian, far removed from the life of the parish—a "head trip," with little heart to be felt in the endless footnotes? It would be wrong to think this—an indication that the reader may not know how long, passionately, and faithfully Barth struggled to preach! As a matter of fact, his lengthy examination of preaching grew out of the weekly obligation and opportunity he encountered as the minister of a parish in Safenwil, Switzerland. Barth was convinced, as he labored with a working-class congregation and shared their social and political concerns, that his primary task was to preach. He believed deeply that people come to church in order to hear again and again, week in and week out, that God is indeed present among them. He was convinced that the whole task of the sermon is to proclaim just that: to state as clearly as possible that God speaks to us in the person of Jesus Christ—that God is present—and to say it so that it might be heard and believed! That was Barth's burden, obligation, and joy. That for him was the purpose of the sermon. Let us see now how he went about this task.

THE IMAGE OF ENCOUNTER

The first thing that strikes one, after reading all Barth's published sermons, is the predominance of a shaping image. It is the image of an encounter. His sermon ideas develop to reveal encounter, a meeting—a confrontation, with one person addressing another. A classic illustration is the sermon "Jesus and Nicodemus."[1] Let us look at the basic structure of that fascinating sermon.

The scene involves a conversation between two people. Nicodemus approaches Jesus by night. Barth imagines the reasons for Nicodemus' inquiry and in this process, describes the human situation as he sees it. Nicodemus is sketched as an intelligent, able seeker, who wants to know more about Jesus. He is drawn because of what he has seen and heard and wishes to engage Jesus in a serious conversation about religion. His concerns are genuine; his needs are real; he is not painted as a superficial person. He comes, hoping to have his questions answered. But Jesus does not comply. Indeed, his response ignores the question entirely. Instead, he says to Nicodemus, "Truly, truly, I say to you, unless one is born anew, he cannot see the kingdom of God" (John 3:3).

The reader or hearer must be shocked. Do not we all have grave concerns to be addressed to Jesus? Do not our inquiries arise out of existential and social frustrations as we struggle to make sense out of life? Barth does not question the seriousness of our needs at all; his respect and admiration for human nature are well documented. Nevertheless, these questions frame our concerns. But they cannot be satisfied by Jesus in this fashion, as if it were his function to provide an answering service for human needs. Therefore—and here the reversal is unmistakeable—it is not Jesus who is to be questioned, but Nicodemus! The tables are now turned; he who addresses is himself addressed; a conversation has become an encounter. The demand Jesus has made is confusing to Nicodemus; he does not know quite how to respond to it. "How can

[one] be born when he is old? Can he enter a second time into his mother's womb and be born?" (John 3:4).

Are not our sympathies with Nicodemus? His literal response to Jesus' figurative language reveals the frustration we all must feel. When have we not read Freud or studied our own attempts to grow and change, without feeling moments of real despair? The impossibility of physical rebirth is an excellent image, then, to describe our own situation—that we repeat our past and cannot climb out of our psychic skins. The grandeur we feel about ourselves and our potential is mingled with the horror we sense when we contemplate our own inhumanity. It is with just this ambiguous view of ourselves that Barth wishes to deal, in the person of Nicodemus. Indeed, it is our view of ourselves and therefore our view of Jesus that must be questioned. Somehow we must come to see ourselves in another perspective. We need to distance ourselves from our conventional images. Then and only then will Jesus' demand be heard! To bring us to this point and to enable us to move outside our own concerns—to enable us to see ourselves through the eyes of Jesus—this is the central point and hope of the sermon.

Now Jesus calls upon Nicodemus to come out from under the roof that blocks his vision of the stars; to cross the river bank that separates them. He assures him that only this decision—this step of faith based solely upon the word of Jesus—will make a new birth possible. Jesus' invitation and demand are both judgment and grace. His judgment descends upon any human attempt to achieve salvation through one's own efforts; his grace is given to those who hear and accept the words of the text, spoken through the sermon, as an encounter with Jesus himself. Jesus is not an illustration or an example of God's grace, but Grace itself! Barth cannot offer more than these words of Jesus; when Jesus speaks to us, God is speaking to us.

So much of what Barth believed and wrote is contained in that one sermon! Indeed, the image of encounter between God and ourselves shapes numerous sermons: "Nevertheless, I Am Continually with Thee," "Saved by Grace," "Look Up to Him," "You Shall Be My People," "He Stands by Us." The subject of these sermons, as proclaimed in the texts, is "God revealed in Jesus Christ." It is God whom we meet in a variety of human situations which evoke questions and concerns, and again and again, the encounter takes on this familiar form.

Let us consider in greater depth the sermon "Be Not Anxious," involving a subject around which countless sermons have been shaped.[2] Barth's style is predictable. With rich insight and deep concern, he paints a vivid picture of our anxiety-ridden lives. He probes below our superficial worries and fears to fathom the deep-rooted care concerning the future that haunts us. But for all this, so movingly set forth, Barth can offer only one response: Be not anxious. In that word is contained all that Barth can say, for in that Word, Jesus himself speaks, offering us his promise that trust in him enables us to live creatively in spite of anxiety. No easy promise is made; and there can be none, because humanly speaking, we cannot think or will our way into some higher anxiety-free existence. We can only trust wholeheartedly in the words spoken to us and in the One who speaks, for they are, in effect, the same. Barth has often stated this conviction, but perhaps nowhere more clearly than in the sermon "Saved by Grace."

> We are gathered here this Sunday morning to hear this word: By grace you have been saved! Whatever else we do, praying or singing, is but an answer to this word spoken to us by God himself—The Bible alone contains this sentence. We do not read it in Kant or in Schopenhauer, or in any book of natural or secular history, and certainly not in any novel, but in the Bible alone. In order to hear this we need what is called the Church—the company of Christians, of human beings called and willing to listen together to the Bible and through it to the Word of God.[3]

THE CENTRALITY OF THE WORD

Let us now look more closely at the assumptions made by Barth which, when fitted together, become the frame in which the sermons are first sketched out and then enfleshed with more detail. When preachers sit before their Bible texts laid out for the coming Sunday, what do they see? What do they expect to read, to contribute, to interpret out of those texts? Clearly, indeed unmistakably, Barth comes to that event as a humble penitent, conscious that before him are the Words of life that speak about God's revelation in Jesus Christ, attested to by the persons who wrote and by the events they describe. To know who God is and what may be said in a given textual situation is repeatedly a discovery, an encounter, and in some profound sense, ever a new event.

This strange book—this Bible—was for Barth a testimony to God's dealings with people. It is not essentially a record of our quest for God, but rather of God's quest, in the person of Jesus Christ, for us. Nowhere else are we told of this movement of God toward us. Nor can God's self-revelation be charted by human reason or discerned from any experience of culture, poetry, or science. God is wholly other than our thoughts. To become involved with the Bible is to enter into a strange new world. Barth never tired of creating images out of this experience. He writes that our situation is like that of a wayfarer who journeys through life "absorbed in his own thoughts and desires," with eyes fixed ahead on the bend in the road—the curve that appears to be the goal sought. This is a familiar world, with all its sights and sounds soothing to the ears, and the traveler retains this sense of well-being until a crisis arises. But occasionally there occurs a foreign word, a sermon that moves him, excites him, and disturbs this ordered life. The bend in the road ahead reveals not a continuation of the way he has been traveling, but a strange new land, "distance undreamed of, a vista he does not see, a place he does not know, the beyond! This new land, shall we seek it? . . . To bring me to this point, to this sign of God's highway, . . . to the end of what is earthly, and so to the beginning of things divine, just this is the aim of every thought and word of the Bible."[4]

This assumption that the Bible is God's revelation of himself in the person of Jesus Christ is Barth's primary act of faith, made not as a form of resignation or as the abdication of reason, but as an act of obedience. One comes to the text and listens, setting aside, as far as is humanly possible, all one's own questions and bracketing one's own assumptions. "Look up to Him, to Jesus Christ. Do not look up to yourselves, or expect when in distress and overcome by life's problems that you can solve them yourselves. Nor can you by scanning the heavens see who it is above who descends and dwells with us. Let him be who he is, above us in heaven. Acknowledge and believe that he is up there and lives for us!"[5]

If "one can come to God only through God himself"; if God is the subject of biblical testimony; if God's self-revelation is available to us only as God chooses to make it known, what then is the task of interpretation? How does one go about understanding what a text has to say? In dealing with this question, we are close to the heart of Barth's faith and the reasons he gives for his own theology. Furthermore, we are able to see clearly how his sermons develop their basic style and form. It is both an act of faith and a dogmatic stance adopted by Barth that God's self-revelation is to be discerned only in the Bible. The Holy Scriptures are a witness—indeed the essential witness—to this revelation. The task of the interpreter, therefore, is one of obedient listening.

This "obedient listening"—what does it mean? Is the interpreter simply a receptacle to be filled by the message the text yields? Does one read, or "listen to," a text without presuppositions? Not at all! We are free decisionmakers, who come to these texts with our own understandings and our own needs. We are all shaped by the world-views and interpretations of texts taught us and accepted by us. These are the tools of the trade that we use to interpret these texts. Furthermore, Barth says we must avail ourselves of gains made in scriptural interpretation, but we must be aware of how we use this higher criticism. No one philosophical system or line of reasoning is normative; a system is only legitimate "and fruitful when it contributes to an understanding of the text. . . . If my mode of thought becomes useful, grace is implied."[6] Obedient listening, then, is to recognize and live with this essential task: being gratefully willing to set aside one's own opinions and understandings and to listen humbly, even though what is being said may profoundly disturb one's own understanding and shatter one's own views of faith. It may change the apparent message of the text or offer disturbing implications for life.

Textual criticism and interpretation for the sake of the sermon (and there can be no subject matter for sermons other than the biblical texts) is itself an encounter. In a way, the encounter between Nicodemus and Jesus typified this event. "Our thoughts must give ground; we cannot free ourselves following the Word of God as a tame beast of prey." The subject of this Word of God is, always and everywhere, Jesus Christ. Texts proclaim his presence, his voice, his judgment, his promise. They speak of his demands upon us and offer only his consolation and guidance. They address us as a demand that must be heard, acceded to, and followed. Textual criticism, then, is the faithful, intelligent quest to hear that Word exposed in the words of the text. "Intelligent comment means that I am driven on till I stand with nothing before me but the enigma of the matter; till the document seems hardly to exist as a document; till I have almost forgotten that I am not its author; till I know the author so well that I allow him to speak in my name."[7] It is as if the task of interpretation were to move beyond the interpretation and live with the writer himself.

How is this leap into the past accomplished? What does it mean to hear these writers so that our hearing becomes a "speaking situation"? Does there not lie between us two thousand years of history? Is there really a sense in which the biblical writers' thoughts and our thoughts may be said to share common assumptions? What analogy makes understanding possible? Barth's primary assumption at this point, and it is crucial to his argument, is that the only analogy available is that of faith. What relates us to Paul, for example, is the shared passion for Christ, the shared acknowledgment that Christ's words are normative for life; that Christ and Christ alone reveals God to us. I cannot emphasize strongly enough the priority of this quest in the interpretation of texts, especially in these particular times, when we are preoccupied with our own situations and look to sermons as means of solving the problems or overcoming the burdens we all carry. We are taught to prepare sermons with the needs of our people in mind. While Barth by no means rejects this concern, his constant insistence is simply that the proper needs and solutions to our problems must take second place. The message of the texts is the gospel of Jesus Christ. Texts do not essentially "contain any instruction about how the world fares or should fare. . . .[They are] the good news of what God is, wants, and does, and is, wants, and does for us." Here again the encounter between Nicodemus and Jesus is central to the argument. Nicodemus' concerns are not dismissed because they are unimportant, but because Nicodemus insists that Jesus respond to his questions, whereas the text makes just the opposite demand: Nicodemus' future depends upon whether he is willing and ready to hear Jesus. What is required of him is not the sacrifice of his thoughts, but their subordination to the words of Jesus.

In all that has gone before, one has the feeling that a wide gulf has been established between the religious seeker and the text. We are told again and again that we cannot grasp God in a net of reason; God's thoughts are not our thoughts. Both God's freedom to speak and the subject matter are, from this point of view, unpredictable: "The wind blows where it will." How then does one hear these words as life-giving testimonies? Here again, Barth is ready with an answer. In a series of sermons devoted to Advent, he discusses the fact that the shepherds heard the glad tidings announced by the angel. "No one can say," he writes, "how it is done. Not even the most devout and learned theologians of all times have been able to give the slightest hint of how one comes to hear the Christmas message. All we can say about hearing the message hinges on the fact that it speaks for itself."[8] The ability to hear these texts speaking of God, to us in our situation, is itself a gift of God—God's gracious impartation of faith, which enables us to receive the announcement of Christ's coming—the Incarnation. Nor is this gift of hearing and responding some kind of resource to be stored up and drawn upon from day to day on a continuous basis. Faith must be found, discovered, and appropriated again and again. Hence there is need for the regular hearing of sermons. It is as if we continually need to be addressed because we lose heart, become weak in faith, and cannot sustain our lives for any length of time, Barth says, unless we are nourished by the words of faith as revealed in the texts.

I have emphasized the activity of the interpreter, or the hearer, and have dwelt upon our attempt to listen to the text and to appropriate what it says. This is our all-too-human but essential response, as preachers and as hearers. It will not, however, enable us to reach the border of our humanity and stand before the edge of eternity. There is no direct path from earth to heaven. Barth does insist that God has indeed traveled in our direction, opened up communication with us, and now dwells in our world. We who seek God must come to believe that God, in the person of Jesus Christ, has sought us out. Christ was not the son of Mary who then became the Son of God, but is the Son of God who became the son of Mary. The Christ who speaks in the texts is not a prophetic figure who in some manner illustrates or exemplifies the ways in which God guides us and shapes our lives; Christ is God speaking—he is God's self-revelation!

All this might seem self-evident to one who believes. But perhaps that assumption is too casual and not reflected upon often enough. In the sermons of Barth, it is the central affirmation. It explains why, as we saw in the sermon "Be Not Anxious," the flow of the argument surges towards one simple, stark, and sufficient source—the words of Jesus, "Be not anxious." "Jesus simply says this without giving a reason for it. . . . It would be something wholly different if Jesus would promise that He will save us from the fiery trial, that He will remove from us the things that give us anxious care. . . . But here one finds nothing of this."[9]

One hardly knows at times where to dip one's bucket and draw up nourishment from the sermonic insights of *Church Dogmatics*, particularly volume 4, because both Barth's sermons and his theological reflections on Christ are passionate, reasoned proclamations of the fact that God reveals himself in these texts. "What else can I say?" he seems to state. "What other than these words?"

> I am at the end. I tried to explain this Bible passage as the word of God fulfilled in Jesus Christ. . . . It then not only says, "I will walk among you," but, "I walk among you." Not only, "I will be your God," but "I am your God." Not only, "You shall be my people," but, "You are my people!" Do you sense the power of this word? The power of him in whom it is fulfilled and becomes a present reality?[10]

It is as if Barth were attempting, with all the skill and commitment at his command, to say that sermons are not about

Christ, but are Christ himself, present here and now, in this congregation, through the presence of the Holy Spirit, and active in the sermon, in both congregation and minister. We who come to church asking, "Is it true that God is present for us?" hear God answering, "Yes, it is true." God's gracious concern for us is revealed in Christ. God is the seeking Father who sends the beloved Son into the world to be set upon and destroyed. Christ's incarnation, death, and resurrection constitute God's humanity among us. His life is the parable, not of the prodigal, but of the obedient son, whose return to the father is greeted with joy. This Christ who comes to us is also he who has dwelt eternally with God. All other images or figures of speech that set aside this basic relationship are human speculations, subject to judgment by the biblical witness.

From the beginning, we have said that the dominant image in Barth's sermons is that of an encounter. We come seeking and are met by One who seeks us; we come asking questions and are rebuffed. Important as our questions are to us, they must be set aside until we have heard what he who speaks to us in the texts has to say. Why this conflict of wills? Are we to believe that Barth is indifferent to our situation? Surely not, for vast sections of content are devoted to an accurate and compassionate description of human pain, sorrow, and misfortune. Furthermore, in sermon after sermon, Barth paid tribute to the grandeur of human potentialities. Nowhere can it be said that Barth rejected accomplishments in the arts or sciences as being unimportant or meaningless. What then is the central problem that Barth believed creates the situation he so often developed in his preaching? It is the human potentiality, and our constant temptation to break the first commandment—to make gods after our own fashion; to fail to acknowledge that we cannot save ourselves—that only One can save us and that to him we owe obedience.

This conviction that we are sinners in need of grace is not dealt with joyfully. There is a brand of preaching in which tone and substance reveal the pleasure the preacher receives from condemning others. None of that may be heard in Barth's sermons; we hear rather the sad and painful sense of life wasted, driven recklessly toward its own ruin in the life of the congregation and also in that of the preacher. In a daring image, Barth preached to prisoners in jail in Basel, saying to them, to himself, and to us as well,

> We are all prisoners. Believe me, there is a captivity much worse than the captivity in this house. There are walls much thicker and doors much heavier than those closed upon you. All of us, the people without and you within, are prisoners of our own obstinacy and pride, of our many greeds, of our various anxieties, of our mistrust and in the last analysis of our unbelief.[11]

The figure shifts, and people are characterized as in need of hope and comfort which they cannot find for themselves or within themselves. Even the church is a community dwelling in darkness and seeking light. One notes an ambiguity throughout these typical descriptions of the human situation. It is as if Barth addressed the church as a community that both knows and does not know its real situation; as if the word of hope and renewed life still echoes somewhere in the regions of consciousness but is blurred and drowned out by the insistent voice of our own self-righteousness —our faith in our ability to solve our own problems. Hence the imperative need to hear the sermon and in its words, to hear and receive the fact of God's presence in Christ.

What is effected in an encounter of this nature? What happens to us when, in humble obedience, confessing our inadequacies, we affirm our utter dependence upon God? In short, what does it mean when we say that we trust completely in the words of Jesus? Then, according to Barth, the miracle takes place. The God who speaks to us in judgment and condemnation is transformed into the God of grace. We discover that God is not angry, and this discovery is experienced as a great joy. "We are lost in amazement and struck by awe, even terror. It is not unlike the experience of Columbus who, sailing for India, suddenly hit upon the continent of America. *This* I did not know. *This* nobody ever told me. *This* I could never have found out for myself—that God is this God, that God does these things."[12] We discover that God's real intention is to have mercy upon us and to empower us to become his people—the church.

Now we are not standing on the other side of the stream of history. We who stood in the relation of adversaries are now friends. He moves into our lives, and this revelation of who God is for us, and who we really are, should evoke in us expressions of great joy. Christians are a people who wear smiles on their faces; their garments are now shining white. They are a people who live, "not in sadness but in joy; not in captivity, but in freedom; not in death, but life."[13]

All this occurs when we accept Jesus as Lord. It is then that we see what we did not perceive before: He who is the humanity of God can become our humanity. Put another way, he tells us who we really are. "The greater the concentration with which we look at Him, the better will be the knowledge that we have of ourselves."[14] His words, "Be not anxious," are no longer words of advice or a moral maxim, but a kind of empowerment, for he now guarantees our future. He becomes our true self: "No longer I, . . . but Christ who lives in me" (Gal. 2:20). Our own needs and concerns are now caught up in the wide range of concerns about the future of the kingdom of God, and we see ourselves as active participants in that calling. What is a Christian community but a "group of people close to Jesus who are with him in such a way that they are directly and unambiguously affected by his promise and assurance"?[15]

Therefore, although the role of judgment in preaching is emphasized in Barth's sermons, the other aspect—the role of grace—is equally emphasized. It is as if the acknowledgment of sin, far from being viewed as a gloomy atmosphere the preacher is to evoke, is actually the prelude to something far more important—the announcement, the promise, the assurance of our redemption and new life together.

The reader undoubtedly will note that for Barth, the primary stress in preaching is the establishment of a right relationship with God. The main subject matter of preaching is not the questions of our daily lives, the needs of our neighbor, or the perils and promises of the world we live in. Indeed one would be tempted to think that ethics played no role in Barth's sermons or in his understanding of the Christian faith itself. His sermons and theological treatises, however, together with his active involvement in the political arena of his age, reveal a much different story. A passionate concern for ethics permeates his writings and dominated his life. But for Barth, true Christian behavior for the sake of the church and the world can be achieved only by a people who regularly, faithfully, and obediently acknowledge their total dependence upon God; who confess that all their works as Christians are empowered by God's grace. Works without faith are dead. Worse yet, they become diabolical. Only God helps. "This means that no thought of our brain, no counsel born of our wisdom; on the whole, no device, no act, no theory, no practice can help—God alone helps. . . . One can only understand this when one's eyes are open, far above all petition and reason, are open for that which helps by Him who helps."[16]

If it is in and through the sermon that help comes to us, and if it is the expectation of the congregation that the sermon, through the effort of the preacher, is to impart that help, then how great is the task laid upon that person! Every Sunday, week in and week out, the dreadful, joyful, necessary, and impossible task awaits the preacher. One must understand that when Barth considered this calling, it is not as though the preacher must somehow, at the last moment, find something to say. Not at all. Preaching is the primary calling of the pastor of a church. But the pastor, too, is in need of grace, in order to preach rightly. The preacher's own unworthiness and incapacities must be acknowledged, for speaking of God is not possible except that God put the words in the preacher's mouth. Therefore—and this is not often stressed—the essential role of prayer in both the preparation and the delivery of the sermon becomes evident. It wells up from a heart and mind saturated with the Bible and overflowing with a life of meditation. "Lord, our God!" begins a prayer before a sermon, "Through thy Son, our Lord Jesus Christ, thou hast made us thy children. We have heard thy voice and have gathered here to give thee praise, to listen to thy word, to call upon thee and to entrust to thy care our burdens and our needs."[17] And after reading the sermon itself, we feel that its entire substance was encapsulated in those passionate pleas. The prayer is the essential mode of address to God—the cry of help for guidance—for there is, in human experience, no other basis for preaching. Hence, "the possibility of knowing the Word of

God lies in the Word of God and nowhere else. Its reality can literally only take place, and as a visible miracle at that."[18]

This then, is Barth's high view of the sermon! It is not too much to say that in Barth's scheme, the sermon effects what the sacrament of the Eucharist offers in Roman Catholic theology: It imparts faith and nourishes life. It is the occasion for faith to be engendered once again in the hearts and minds of the congregation. In and through the words of the preacher, who is caught up in the Spirit, God in Christ is recognized as truly being present.

AN APPRAISAL

Reading both Barth's sermons and his theological writings (and they belong together), one is deeply impressed and moved by his passion, piety, and profundity of thought. He lived and wrote during an era dominated by what he called liberalism, at a time when the church tended to support the ideological structure of the state and received protection and support in return. In this process, the church lost its capacity to think for itself and was unable to develop a self-understanding out of its own history and faith. Barth attacked what he called religion, meaning the church's tendency to be preoccupied with itself, to be self-righteous, to make an idol of itself. He believed that the first commandment had been broken and that God's sovereignty and freedom had been severely circumscribed. In short, he feared that theology had become another expression of anthropology. He stood against the stream; he denied all human attempts to encompass God or to use God.

Our debt of gratitude to Barth is tremendous. In the last analysis, it is he who directs us again and again to remember the unique possibility in preaching: that God will speak to us of life in Jesus Christ. It is God who takes the initiative. It is this Word of life we need to hear and that we must hear.

One is forced to ask, however, if language about God is not, after all, human language, and if the language Barth uses—the language of the Bible—is not itself part of the problem of communication between ourselves and God. The basic image that informs the religious story is that of a descending/ascending deity, dear to Christianity for almost two thousand years and attested to in creeds and religious art. It is this aesthetic expression that is seriously questioned in our age by people for whom the cosmological world-view that shaped it is no longer believable. Indeed, the first attack upon Barth's theology was by his contemporary, Rudolf Bultmann, who, as early as 1925, published an essay entitled "How Is It Possible to Speak of God Today?" His thesis centers not so much on the category of "faith," as Barth develops it, but upon "understanding." It is Bultmann's contention that biblical language, burdened by mythological images, must be decoded. He argues that ancient and modern peoples differ in their views of the nature of the universe, but that they share the same experiences of guilt, dread, fear of death, and anxiety about the future. These categories of human existence are available to us not only in the New Testament but in contemporary existential philosophy. One must therefore scrape off the husks of mythological language to discern the real questions that gave it birth. Thus Bultmann's sermons address us as contemporaries of the New Testament, seeking to show us how we are gripped by the same issues they struggled with. It is only when we come to the point of understanding who we really are, that we can begin to hear the message of a text. In a way, then, knowledge about God must begin with a kind of self-knowledge—a self-awareness—that makes it possible for us to believe. The sermon becomes a time of identity crisis and enhances the possibility of hearing anew the words of life. Thus it follows that the proper point of departure in preaching is not with God, but with our own situation, in order that we may hear God speaking.

One other issue to be reflected upon has to do with the tendency of Barth's theology to make a sharp and absolute distinction between God and ourselves. True enough, as Barth never tires of reminding us, we do not carry God around in our vest pockets, drawing upon a power that is captive to our felt needs. Nevertheless, are there not other legitimate ways to read and understand the biblical story? Are we not called to be stewards of the earth, and have we not been baptized into a faith that finds expression in an altogether human life-style? We may well say with Paul, "Not I, but Christ who lives in me," and recognize the real distinction. Do we not already have some knowledge of God's redeeming presence among us? It may be that the sharp distinction between nature and history is overdrawn.

It is certainly true that the questions raised in this age are different from those that occupied the center of Barth's attention. We seek today to find a "gracious neighbor," and together to find some way to preserve existence in the face of the almost daily threat of extinction to our planet. Our movement in the religious quest is more horizontal than vertical, not necessarily out of pride and vainglory, but in the legitimate attempt to establish a new life-style in our world. It is not that Barth's theology is anachronistic, so much as that it offers too little guidance for the very human endeavor to exist in a future with contours largely unknown and filled with as much dread as hope.

II. EXISTENTIALISM: PAUL TILLICH

Love is "the power of reconciliation whose work is wholeness."

Paul Tillich

When reading or listening to the sermons of Paul Tillich, one soon becomes aware of a basic motif—reconciliation, or reunion. In Tillich's preaching, the individual, torn from within and without, is invited to become whole again. It is important to note that word *again*, for our disorder is a sign not only of our experience of anxiety, frustration, and meaninglessness, but it is also the echo, or recollection, of our real state of being. It is as though the answer to our questions about life's purpose and goal is, in some ambiguous, hidden manner, already known to us. In the restless search for wholeness, health, and self-fulfillment, we may sense our awareness of the absence of God; our thirst suggests that we once drank deeply at the well of being. The intention of sermons, therefore, is to enable us to penetrate the surface features of daily life, to recognize our situation, and to affirm a power at work in us.

The encounter so clearly developed in Barth's sermons—the God who comes to us in Jesus Christ, from beyond into the midst of life—is now an encounter taking place *within* us, fully manifested in Jesus the Christ, but at work in our lives as well. We are told in Tillich's sermons that we cannot accept the presence of Christ until we accept ourselves, work through the strife and discord that rends us apart, and lay hold of the inner power that we have forgotten, ignored, or consciously rejected. We are invited to look within, more than to look up. We are urged to take seriously the clues to our real situation, not only as they come to us in judgment through the biblical texts, but also as they are mediated in the arts, in science, in other religions—in the widest sense, in culture itself.

If Barth has told us, in the encounter between Nicodemus and Jesus, that we who have questions about religion and life's meaning must first listen to Jesus and accept his interpretation of our real problems, Tillich consciously begins at the other end. Nicodemus' concerns are ultimate; they must be viewed with the utmost thoughtfulness. Therefore, Tillich's sermons begin with Nicodemus and attempt to demonstrate how he may find within himself the resources to which Jesus speaks. "Being born again" may be stated more meaningfully as "becoming whole again." In general terms, if Barth calls us to begin our quest with God as revealed in Jesus Christ, Tillich calls us to begin with ourselves—to discover that it is ultimately true that Jesus Christ is the final revelation of a power at work even now in ourselves and, indeed, in all creation.

Here are clearly differing ideas as to how faith is mediated, differing understandings of the human predicament, and differing views of the nature and purpose of the sermon. This is not surprising, since Tillich made his disagreements with Barth amply clear, maintaining that in the final analysis, Barth's God is unavailable to us and that Barth's theology does more to obscure and prevent communion with God than to make that encounter possible. Let us now look at Tillich's sermons and other writings, to understand his beliefs and to see how his sermons reflect his theology of preaching.

NAMING THE ETERNAL

In his sermon "The Yoke of Religion," based upon the passage in Matthew's Gospel, "Come to me, all who labor and are heavy laden" (11:28), Tillich argues that the "yoke," or burden, that oppresses people is religion itself.[1] The sermon seeks to show that Jesus offers us release from this burden and a new life. "Religion"—and here we must note carefully how that word is being used by Tillich—is assent to a variety of doctrines and creedal statements, which, as they are presently taught or expounded in sermons, bear little resemblance to our understanding of our predicament or to their own source. In short, the language of

Christian faith, as it is now used, is itself a yoke, a burden like the Law, offering what it cannot give. "People," he writes elsewhere, "know the dimension of the eternal, but they cannot accept our names for it."[2] That being the case, the aim of the sermon is to evoke in the hearts and minds of the congregation a new process for understanding how faith is received, recognized, and affirmed. To enable this evocation, preacher and congregation are called upon to think through the traditional religious language in order to locate the power it contains—a power that is obscured by the names we assign to it. The quest for this kind of religious insight carries us through an examination of the words, and an examination of ourselves as well, to discover how the questions we ask about the meaning of our lives can be answered. Ultimately, it is the purpose of the sermon to make us aware that the "new being" in and through whom we ourselves may become reconciled, healed, and made whole, is manifested in Jesus Christ.

The central theme of the sermon contains most of the elements that characterize Tillich's form and style and also reveals his underlying assumption concerning the human situation, the way in which texts are used, and the philosophical and theological premises that undergird that process and support the sermons themselves. Let us begin with Tillich's interpretation of our situation today, for this interpretation of who we are and what we seek is central to both his method and his message.

THE AGE OF ANXIETY

Our situation today may be epitomized in the observation that we live in the Age of Anxiety. People experience a lack of meaning in their lives and are painfully aware of this condition, whatever words they may use to describe it. Terms such as "emptiness," "estrangement," and "the awareness of finitude," familiar to existential thought, appear frequently in the sermons, as they do elsewhere in Tillich's writings. His book *The Courage to Be* has become a classic description of the concept of anxiety as applied to both the religious and the secular situation of this age.[3] This sign of our age is disclosed in science, art, politics, psychiatry, and religion, as well. It appears not only in an anxiety born of fear that we have transgressed God's laws, but in a pervading sense throughout life of "dis-ease," disorder—of fragmentation and restlessness. The surface forms of anxiety expressed in neurotic behavior point to an internal sense of emptiness and, although ambiguously sensed, a quest for meaning. The feeling that life lacks purpose, direction, or goal is pervasive and points to the felt need to become whole again; to move from dis-ease to health.

In our plight, we sometimes turn to psychiatrists to help us work through our repressions and to enable us to be liberated from "demons" that rage in our lives. Helpful and necessary as that may be, ultimately neither psychiatrist nor counselor can make us whole, for there is an anxiety still deeper than that revealed by their analytic skills. It is the anxiety about life's meaning itself, to which these other anxieties finally point. It is reality itself that we encounter in this inner depth of life—reality appearing before us as both threat and promise, creativity and destruction, love and hate.

> Who heals reality? Who brings us a new reality? Who reconciles the conflicting forces of our whole existence? . . .Who heals the healer? . . . It is the humanly incredible, ecstatic, often defeated, but never conquered faith of Christianity that this new reality which was always at work in history, has appeared in fullness and power in Jesus the Christ, the Healer, the Savior.[4]

What we see at work here is the conscious attempt to bring together two understandings of the human situation—ontology and the Christian faith—and to show how they complement each other, or how one points to the other as its fulfillment. These are not separate pursuits of meaning going their own ways. The new reality, Jesus the Christ, has always been at work in history. What the biblical texts proclaim is that he who has come and is proclaimed in the texts is the final expression of the quest of all creation. Therefore, all people, regardless of what faith they espouse, and even those who reject commitment to any faith, are nevertheless fundamentally motivated by some final, ultimate concern which shapes their lives. In the sense that this quest is the search for meaning and unification, it may properly be called a religious concern.

In a sermon titled "The Theologian," which has for its text Acts 17:22-34—Paul's sermon addressed to people who believe in an "unknown God"—Tillich argues that Paul's strategy is to demonstrate that those who seek an unknown God are not unconscious of the answer.[5] In asking the question, one in a sense already participates in, or is aware of, the vital importance of the answer. This being the case, a sermon is frankly apologetic. Thus for Tillich, "To defend oneself before an opponent with a common criterion in view . . . the decisive question of ancient and modern apologetics is that of a common criterion, the court of judgment where the dispute can be settled."[6]

The acceptance of Christ as Savior or Healer is hindered not by the lack of faith, but by the language used to present faith. If we are to communicate with people today in their world, we must so state the situation as to enable them "to decide for or against it." Therefore, one essential task of the sermon is to revive moribund religious language and to be willing, when necessary, to discard it altogether, in favor of language more meaningful to this age. This is not to say that there is no specific religious language, but rather that the language used, the so-called jargon, is not simply a shorthand used within the profession—the kind one hears in seminary halls and lecture rooms; it is language that obscures understanding in both seminaries and sanctuaries. We are then dealing here with two related issues in communication: language and experience. Let us see how Tillich handles these in his sermons, beginning with language—religious language.

LANGUAGE AS COMMUNICATION

Tillich maintains that religious language is fundamentally symbolic. By "symbol," Tillich refers to a word or an image that points to our ultimate concern and evokes in us an awareness of the "beyond in the midst of life." A symbol, to use Tillich's well-known analogy, is like a stained-glass window, in that it is transparent to the light. It is the light shining upon it and through it that gives it meaning and attracts us. The symbol is necessary for this illumination, but solely as a means of pointing beyond itself to the reality of light. It serves, then, as a means of disclosure. Such symbols, he argues, are not made but apparently are born, or emerge, and are recognized as appropriate. The phrase "Black is beautiful" is typical; it has served as a symbolic disclosure of their basic identity to millions of Americans, in a world that for centuries has denied their worth as black people. The symbol is a moment of disclosure that at times has been called a speech-event—a luminous clarification of life. Tillich maintains that the final test of the adequacy of religious symbols is "whether or not they are able to communicate something infinitely important to us."

What language is available to us today that will point to its ultimate source of power and at the same time touch us at the level of our ultimate concern? In Tillich's view this inquiry is essential; his sermons abound with examples of experiments with new language forms. For many people, he argues, even the word "God" no longer communicates the power to which it has pointed in times gone by, because that word has become an object of knowledge, with a meaning or reference shaped by a world-view that no longer is thinkable for us. One must bear in mind that religious language is culture-bound. Its power to reveal is necessarily limited by the thought-forms of the age in which it appeared. Furthermore, religious language shaped by the Gospels has itself been reshaped and reinterpreted by succeeding ages. For example, many people find that when they employ the word God to express their ultimate concern, the symbol is associated at once in their minds and imaginations with spatial connotations that are both inevitable and confusing. Granting that language, since it is a human creation, is unavoidably shaped by relations of time and place, it is nevertheless true that the use of the word God fails to overcome the tendency to think of God as "out there" or "up there." God then becomes an object of thought, a being alongside other beings. Such an interpretation of the word empties God of mystery and sovereignty. When we experience this phenomenon and are puzzled by or even estranged from this designation, it might be better to discard the word and to speak of God as "that unknown force that makes us restless." Or we may have to wait expectantly, in an attitude of prayer, for new words to emerge.

Unwillingness to use such words may of course express our doubt, as well. But doubt, for Tillich, is a legitimate and necessary characteristic of faith. It is the other side, implied in faith itself. It does not necessarily point to a glaring fault in our lives, but rather indicates that we no longer experience the power of religion to seize us and make us whole when such language is used. Knowing the name; learning the creed; acquiring the necessary knowledge about God may be at best an assent to religious faith, and may constitute, in itself, a barrier to real communion with God.

Are there symbols alive and at work in our culture today that may become bearers of religious insight? In Tillich's view, two of these terms, "sickness" and "health," are in wide use today, particularly as expressed in psychosomatic medicine. "Sickness," as Tillich employs the symbol, points to the divided, disfunctioning, fragmented nature of existence, while "health" points to the potential and essential need for unification or wholeness. Indeed, in an address to the graduating class at Union Theological Seminary in New York City, he called for a ministry of healing, arguing that healing is an adequate symbol for communicating the gospel in this age. The related traditional religious terms are "sin" and "salvation." Indeed, it may become necessary to discard the word sin, for it is commonly and almost universally associated with moral actions against the law. When this interpretation prevails, the symbol has lost its power to communicate its original meaning of that basic cleavage in our existence. "Salvation," in this tradition, tends to denote the decision to obey the law, or to give up smoking or swearing. When this interpretation shapes our understanding of such language, then the original power of the word salvation is lost, for it once meant healing, or wholeness, or health, and pointed to the total reconstitution of oneself. Many of Tillich's sermons are devoted to the attempt to preserve religious language, to enable people to reinterpret the words so that their symbolic depth becomes clear once again.

Tillich believed that the age in which Jesus lived, like our own time, ascribed the terms "sickness" and "disease" not only to bodily ailments, but also to what we today would call psychic disorder. The term used for this ailment was "demon possession." Tillich believed that Jesus described his own ministry as one of healing: "This is what he says: 'If I am able to heal the deaf and blind, if I am able to liberate the mentally sick, then a new reality has come upon you.' "[7]

In keeping with his conviction that the power to make us whole is manifested in all reality, Tillich maintains that psychiatrists who diagnose and treat neuroses, understood in this way as modern forms of demon possession, participate in the power of wholeness or being and are themselves bearers of its power. "Wholeness," understood as "health" in the New Testament, however, has a wider connotation and is mediated only through Christ. For what fundamentally destroys existence is not psychic illness; this disease is a manifestation of a deeper power at work in us, experienced as estrangement from the self. That is what sin finally is. Thus the psychic disorders of our time, which tear us apart within and also manifest themselves in our culture and civilization, point to a common human situation. Tillich interprets the narrative of the Fall in Genesis in just these terms, in order to awaken in us the ability to be moved by its profound symbolic meaning so that it may once again address us. The Fall resulted in what is called "self loss" or the "disintegration of the unity of the person," or the "horrifying experience of falling to pieces."[8] The Fall symbolizes our awareness of estrangement from ourselves, as well as our struggle for self-reconciliation and reunion.

Sickness is a universal experience within the church, attested to, but often denied. "Every minister," writes Tillich, "who is proud of a smooth-running or gradually growing church should ask himself whether or not such a church is able to make its members aware of their sickness, and to give them the courage to accept the fact that they are healed."[9]

In order to awaken in us a true sense of our situation and open us to the powers of healing mediated in Jesus the Christ, Tillich attempts a wide-ranging reinterpretation of a number of traditional religious terms. These are scattered throughout the sermons and dealt with in greatest detail in volume 3 of his *Systematic Theology*. When the sermons and theological reflections are read together, one senses a conscious attempt to apply the reflection to the sermon. Let us look at one such symbol and its implications for preaching.

The symbol "resurrection" is developed in many ways. It is that situation—that encounter with the new reality in Christ—in which one is overtaken or overpowered by a presence that organizes and gives meaning to life. This wholeness of life is an ever-present possibility, and "resurrection's" use and power are limited when applied solely to some future existence after death or when connected with the idea of immortality of the soul. Resurrection is the eternal now; it is the presence of the Infinite with us in time and finitude; it is a new life lived out under the conditions of existence; it is experienced as the unleashing of creative powers. It is therefore "health," or "salvation," and in that sense it is a present expression of the meaning of reality, both in the present and in the future. The whole of life appears reintegrated, and therefore resurrection is a reconciliation and reunion with ourselves, with God, and with nature.

One dimension of this new understanding of the meaning of existence is the experience of forgiveness. For "nothing greater can happen to a human being than that he is forgiven. For forgiveness means reconciliation in spite of estrangement; it means reunion in spite of hostility."[10]

"Forgiveness," and "acceptance" as its necessary precondition, are related symbols pointing to profound psychic needs in our nature. We may witness the truth of this experience on the contemporary scene in the spiritual odyssey of both whites and blacks in America. White people's acceptance of themselves is rejected by the black community. "White people," writes James Baldwin, "cannot in generality be taken as models of how to live. Rather the white man is himself in sore need of new standards which will release him from his confusion and place him once again in fruitful communion with the depths of his own being."[11] The question is, however, What must occur in order that a healthful self-acceptance can take place? It cannot be expected from blacks, whose self-esteem has been systematically destroyed, although many whites hope for just that solution. They wish to let bygones be bygones, erase the past, and start afresh. The attempt to demonstrate a viable way of reconciliation found public expression in the strategies of Martin Luther King, Jr. The nonviolent philosophy he developed into a political force was an attempt to accept the unacceptable, to love the unlovable; but it has been largely rejected by the black community.

When white people turn to religion as a source of forgiveness in this kind of situation, they tend, as human beings, to filter out the element of judgment implicit in their behavior. They tend to justify themselves in order to preserve a false image of themselves. They cannot fundamentally accept themselves and consequently cannot accept blacks who demand to be accepted as equals. They cannot live, because they have not died. They cannot be raised from their dead condition, because they have not been buried. They cannot accept the love of God, because they hear their own voices of condemnation and do not hear God's word of acceptance "in spite of."

Tillich believes that there are moments when "one is grasped by a human face as human, although one has to overcome personal distaste or racial strangeness or national conflict."[12] There are moments when forgiveness invades our existence like a fire that both burns and heals, and we experience reconciliation with ourselves and are able to accept ourselves and others. These "saving events" traditionally are occurrences in the context of the Christian church, "where the reunion of man with man is an actual event," or at least an ever-present possibility. If it does not take place there, it well may be experienced in other structures of our life—perhaps even more in situations of hostility where anger and agony are fully exposed. For the fierceness of emotions and their furious expression in the heat of confrontation is both a catharsis and a confession. In such situations broken images and self-delusions may die.

Another related symbol is that of "death." In our time as in every age, we need to know something that is stronger than death. We find ourselves speaking of the decay and death of cities, of the pollution of our natural environment, and of the "balance of terror" built into our contemporary armaments race, with its overkill possibilities. No one has seen the presence of death more clearly than the modern scientist. In warning us of the potential destructiveness in hydrogen power, the scientist tells "this generation what the prophets told their generations: that earth and man, trees and animals, are threatened by a catastrophe which they can scarcely escape."[13]

Death symbolizes not only our destructive capacities in psychological and physical terms; it also symbolizes the tragic depth of existence itself. It is not so much that we fear the natural death of all things; we rebel against it at a deeper level because we are aware of death as the extinction of being—as the ultimate expression of meaninglessness. This awareness of what Tillich calls our finitude is prompted by the Infinite with which we seek reunion and is expressed in various religious yearnings for immortality. "Only because we are able to see the eternal can we see the limited time that is given us. Only because we can elevate ourselves above the animals can we see that we are like animals. Our melancholy about our transitoriness is rooted in our power to look beyond it."[14]

Tillich believes there are moments when we are grasped and shaped by an event that moves us fundamentally, so that we stand outside ourselves and are overcome by the realization that each moment of life is also an occasion for eternal life. In such moments traditional understandings of the terms life and death are transcended by the ultimate question, To be or not to be? This understanding of the meaning of our lives is revealed in the words of Jesus: "Whoever would save his life will lose it; and whoever loses his life for my sake, he will save it" (Luke 9:24). This life of which Jesus speaks has nothing to do with the idea of survival in the hereafter, but is life in the sense of finding the pearl of great price, an event that carries ultimate concern and meaning for us.

To be grasped by this understanding is to be overcome by the providence of God. Here again we come upon Tillich's determined effort to revive a traditional religious term. "Providence" is not to be understood as a divine plan or design made before the world began, determining our lives so that we fulfill our predetermined destiny.

Such a popular use of this symbol ignores the element of contingency that characterizes history and bypasses our freedom to shape our own destinies. Furthermore, it prejudges and determines the way God must act. We have lost the original definition, and the real depth of that symbol is no longer available to us. "Neither the personal nor the historical belief in providence had depth or a real foundation. These beliefs were products of wishful thinking and not of faith."[15]

What then does providence mean? Tillich says that it is "the courage to say yes to one's own life and life in general, in spite of the driving forces of fate, in spite of the insecurities of daily existence, in spite of the catastrophies of existence and the breakdown of meaning."[16] In fact, as Tillich states it, providence is faith itself, expressed as the courage to affirm life and born of the assurance that nothing can separate us from the love of God—or in Tillich's terms, "the ultimate victory over separation." When the individual accepts this understanding of God through an act of commitment, a form of certainty is experienced—not as a self-certainty but as an understanding of life. Faith is realizing that we do not possess God as an object of knowledge; that our doctrines and creeds are at best pointers, and often misdirections; and that therefore we strive in vain for certainty. It is recognizing that our moments of ecstasy are followed by periods of despair and that we move into and out of faith. Faith, then, is not contained in ourselves or in our ability to be certain of the meaning of our lives, but is rather a constant and firm belief that God is with us; that he is the power conferring ultimate meaning to our lives.

EXPERIENCE AS COMMUNICATION

Throughout this rather brief introduction to Tillich's attempt to reinterpret religious language, the reader will have noted his frequent appeals to the congregation's experience. He tells us that we have had experiences when we were grasped, shaken, and reconciled. This is a cardinal point in Tillich's quest for meaningful language. Our own experience is to be viewed with the utmost seriousness, not only in our awareness of its ability to deceive us, but also with the realization that often it is, or may be interpreted as, the presence of God. Such experiences are not without the dimension of the eternal. For example, expressions of gratitude that spontaneously form on our lips—words that "lack a definite object towards which to turn"—reveal that "thankfulness has taken hold of us, not because something special has happened to us, but just because we are, because we participate in the glory and power of being. . . . It is a state of being."[17] To be overcome by this understanding of existence, which at first well may lack any definable or nameable object, is in itself a way to give glory to God. "An unbeliever who is filled with thanks for his being has ceased to be an unbeliever. His rejoicing is a spontaneous obedience to the exhortation of our text—'Rejoice always.' "[18]

In developing the implications of the text "The fear of the Lord is the beginning of knowledge" (Prov. 1:7), Tillich says that the insights of the ages, expressed in wisdom literature, in culture, and in religion, witness to life's mystery, to the tragic dimensions of existence; in so doing, they testify to the boundary line of human existence—that is, the awareness of finitude. One stands before the abyss of existence. To be aware of this experience of life is to be grasped by an ultimate concern, and this awareness and acknowledgment direct us toward the deepest implications of the event.

In the same manner, our quest for truth symbolizes our fundamental need, traceable throughout our lives. As we struggle with this haunting concern, we may come to learn that truth is not the acquisition of knowledge, but is a form of self-liberation in the deepest sense—a freeing from the bonds of prejudice, opinion, and convention. We learn that the truth is not in us, though we desperately long for its presence. In moments of clarity—those lucid moments that dawn upon us—we are overwhelmed by insights about ourselves, insights that have a healing, integrative effect upon our self-understanding. The final truth to which these truths point is Jesus the Christ, who is himself the Truth. "Many at all times and in all places have encountered the true reality which is in him without knowing the name—as he himself said. They were of the truth and they recognized the truth, although they had never seen him who is the truth."[19]

In a moving sermon entitled "Spiritual Presence," Tillich insists that experiences of emptiness and meaninglessness; or the awakening desire to fill the void; or the determination to say yes to life; or the promptings that encourage us to return love for hate or that liberate us from our own bondage to vengefulness towards others, are, whether we know their source or not, signs of the presence of God. The tragic fact is, Tillich believes, that the traditional language we use to describe these real events in our lives does more to conceal than to disclose who we really are. If these words fail us, Tillich invites us to gaze without words at the figure of Christ. In him we see the Spirit and the Life fully revealed.

Precisely who is this Spirit and Life? Here we come to Tillich's understanding of the Bible and to the way he exegetes texts for the purpose of preaching: He reads texts both as a philosopher and as a theologian. In fact, if we understand him correctly, one cannot and ought not do otherwise if one wishes to address people today. Indeed, the use of existential language and the drawing upon insights of culture, art, and science, aid us in the task of becoming familiar with the texts. For example, on the level of philosophical assertion, Tillich states that Jesus as the Christ "represents the essential unity between God and Man appearing under the conditions of existential estrangement."[20]

"Estrangement" is Tillich's term to describe our awareness of separation from ourselves, while "unity" describes our quest for wholeness. In Jesus Christ, we see before us One who, under the conditions of estrangement, was so grasped by God and so completely oriented toward God, that in and through Christ, God is fully revealed as the Power that brings life together and unifies it. The Gospel accounts record the powers of estrangement that confronted him, and before which he did not succumb. Tillich refers to the events of the crucifixion as making this clear, for even then at the moment of death, when life's meaninglessness is our common experience, Christ did not deny but rather affirmed his complete faith in God. He thus manifests in himself an undisrupted union with God and is in himself the perfect expression of that power. Jesus the Christ, then, is the New Being; he is the perfection toward which all existence moves. He is in this sense the final revelation for us of who God is—the One toward whom all creation moves and all religions point.

It is important to note that Tillich consistently refers to Jesus as "the Christ," or as "Jesus the Christ." The insertion of the definite article is, it seems to me, a calculated one. Tillich makes a distinction between the Jesus of history and Jesus the Christ of faith, arguing that it is the saving power manifested in his presence that grasps us in biblical texts and that makes sense to us in our age. Jesus as a person is not an object of faith. It is not his teachings or moral admonitions that constitute his charisma, but his very being.

This method of reading the texts is largely unfamiliar to contemporary western Protestant eyes. We tend to emphasize the words and deeds of Jesus in our teaching and preaching. He is variously a psychologist, an ethical teacher, or a revolutionary, calling us to transform society into a political expression of the kingdom of God. Tillich, on the other hand, asks us to see Jesus in the Gospel accounts as a figure similar to the icons created in stone, mosaics, and metal by the artists of the Byzantine and Romanesque eras. When one contemplates those religious objects, one is aware that the human features and the so-called lineaments of the figures function solely to mediate the power and glory of a force or an energy that is behind them and shines through them. Those figures are symbols. Their power of attraction is not in themselves, but in what they point to. They exist or were created for that purpose. They evoke feelings of awe and reverence, as if they contained power or were manifestations of holiness.

The humanity of Jesus the Christ is not denied as if he had been a phantom, or as if he never had been a real human being who suffered in all things as we suffer. Nevertheless, in Tillich's sermons there is a tendency to stress the divine dimension of Jesus. The unity, or indivisibility of Jesus Christ as both Man and God, symbolized in the doctrine of the Trinity and confessed in the Nicene Creed, is strained. Thus for example, when John the Baptist sends emissaries to ask if he really is the Messiah, Jesus responds by saying that the sick are healed, the dead raised, and the lepers cleansed. All these are signs of the presence of the kingdom—that is, of the presence of a power that heals life. It is, according to Tillich, the recognition of the presence of this power that assuages John the Baptist's doubts. That this power is manifested in Jesus is almost of secondary importance. Here again, one senses the striving to get behind or beyond the person of Jesus; to make contact with the power emanating from his presence.

Jesus, then, is not in himself an object of faith. "None of His superior qualities—neither His religious life nor His moral perfection nor his profound insights make Him an object of faith."[21] Indeed, Jesus himself cautions people not to ascribe to him some ultimate authority or to believe in him as an object of faith. He does not speak on his own authority, but points people to the Authority and Power that has sent him and to whom he testifies. When we make Jesus an object of faith, he becomes trapped and limited by our time-bound categories of thought, as well as by our need to make him as we are. It is only as we see in him the full expression of the Father that he becomes Jesus the Christ for us. According to Tillich, "Nothing is left in the face of Jesus the Christ which is only Jesus of Nazareth, which is only the face of one individual beside others."[22]

All Tillich's published sermons are based upon texts that are as carefully exegeted, commented upon, and developed as are the structures of the sermons themselves. It is to be noted however, that his choice of texts is selective and the messages they offer tend to be much the same. They all, in one manner or another, direct our thought and reflection to the fundamental need to locate a power of renewal and to sense in the texts themselves the availability of that power for our lives today. This should not surprise us, since the preacher's own theological and philosophical concerns constitute the glasses through which the texts are read.

AN APPRAISAL

Many preachers have been deeply influenced by Tillich's sermons and by his other writings as well. They share his feeling that religious language no longer communicates to people in this age. They agree that if such language does not speak to us in some powerful, captivating sense, it must either be discarded, or in some fashion translated anew into terms that we can understand. Others applaud his investigations into psychiatry and the arts and share with him the belief that culture is not without manifestations of the power to heal life, or at least, as in contemporary art forms, to point prophetically to the illnesses of our age. Many ministers who have been trained for counseling find Tillich's insistence that human experience is to be regarded with the utmost seriousness congenial to their professional work. That experience in its fragmented, conflicting, and painful presence, is not only a sign of our inner discord; it possesses positive, healing dimensions, as well. Finally, the structure of Tillich's sermons has been used by many as a welcome alternative to a sermon that tends to tell people who they are and what they must believe, as if it offered the final truth about life. Tillich's method is to evoke questions or to enable his hearers to examine themselves more closely, more realistically, more honestly. He tends to function as a guide who walks along the path of self-examination with us, sharing the struggle to become whole once again. He considers us thoughtfully, and as a good therapist, provides the atmosphere for us to reevaluate ourselves and the way in which Christian faith can answer our genuine concerns. The mood of the sermons is one of contemplation, and they call us to fulfill our potential. The general tendency is to invite us to "become," not to "do." For unless we are reunited within ourselves, we cannot act in a healthful, healing fashion, either in terms of our own personal lives or in our relations with our neighbors.

There are, however, some serious questions one must put to these sermons, and they center on one's own theological beliefs, one's own understanding of the biblical message concerning Jesus Christ, and the form in which it may be communicated today. For example, it may be well to question whether many of Tillich's terms are any more clear than the language used in the texts. One is assailed by an existentially oriented vocabulary. Terms such as alienation, finitude, being, and becoming—and, indeed, the key term, new being—cry out for clarity. If Tillich argues that the symbol "God" has lost its power to communicate meaning today, it might be asked if the description of Christ as the New Being helps matters a great deal.

Is Tillich's analysis of the human situation, apart from its function as a key to interpretation of texts, accurate? Is not existentialistic philosophy peculiar to Western thought and associated primarily with a political and social situation of this age? Many critics argue that existentialism is far too preoccupied with the individual and his or her inner pilgrimage, to the neglect of the social and political life we all lead. Inner reconciliation is not a process to be carried out in solitude and contemplation apart from one's participation in the common life. We cannot, in fact, understand ourselves unless we see ourselves in that context. Thus Tillich's tendency to assign a subordinate role to the teachings and deeds of Jesus seems out of place. Furthermore, the sermons do not, in any direct way, challenge us to participate in the struggles for human dignity, justice, and peace in the world. Indeed, the whole category of the future and the coming of the kingdom of God is muted. The sermons are more therapeutic than prophetic in nature. The reunification of life is an event that can occur in the "eternal now"; it is made possible when the past is overcome and we are made new. But the "new" is the realization of what has been lost through the fragmentation of life. Thus the direction of faith and hope is more toward the past then toward the future; more toward a recovery of what we once were than the discovery of and anticipation of a genuinely new future.

Granting the necessity and the obligation to raise such questions as well as others that may strike us as we read, it is still true that the sermons bear the stamp of an original, questing mind. Their probing, iconoclastic, and some would say, heretical nature are courageous attempts to enable people to hear the good news of the gospel once again.

III. LIBERALISM: THE AMERICAN SCHOOL

We would be building . . . temples still undone.
                                                    Purd E. Deitz

In 1926, a volume of essays by Harry Emerson Fosdick was published under the title *Adventurous Living*, expressing his understanding of the issues that perplexed and challenged religious thinkers in seminaries and churches. He set forth his response to those issues in what he called a liberal theology, cautioning his readers not to press that term too hard, since it was somewhat hazy and ambiguous. He feared that people who termed themselves liberal might be found following many doctrinal banners—"swashbuckling radicals, believing not much of anything, to men of well-established convictions who are tolerant of differences and open-minded to new truth." What did unite liberals, however, were certain aims which he summarized as follows: "To think the great faiths of the Gospel through in contemporary terms, and to harness the great dynamics of the Gospel to contemporary tasks."[1]

That basic interest is revealed in a substantial body of published sermons preached during that period. Indeed, the sermons of Fosdick are still read, and their influence is still heard and felt in many pulpits today. Ministers who feel themselves rooted in this tradition of preaching cross denominational lines and creedal differences. What they all share is the concern expressed by Fosdick: How may the gospel be preached today in such a manner that its power to change society and the world may be heard, understood, and appropriated? Here again, as in all the chapters of this book, specific cultural and theological concerns shape the question and the answers. The reader may find, as we examine what the liberals strove for and fought against, that their issues and passionate enthusiasms are ours as well. It is important then to examine the era in which they lived, to see how their theology of preaching developed from the impulse to summon people to a joyful, obedient discipleship in Christ.

We begin with a brief synopsis of a sermon by Fosdick, "The Sacred and the Secular Are Inseparable," found in James W. Cox's edition of *The Twentieth-Century Pulpit*. Fosdick laments the fact that religion and reality have been growing farther and farther apart. People struggle daily with the great issues of a modern age about which religion has little to say. Religious life is increasingly ghettoized and absorbed in private, doctrinal matters and hairsplitting arguments about the nature of Christ and the church. The language and the matters debated seem far removed from our real concerns today. God has been pushed into a corner of our world at a time when the participation of religion in daily life is desperately needed. Jesus, whose deeds were carried out in the everyday round of existence, has become an object of creedal interpretation, remote and almost hidden from our consciousness. Worse still, a whole generation of young people is growing up more and more alienated from religion. What is needed, then, is a religion that overcomes that growing split between the sacred and the secular—a "secularized Christianity," a faith for the living of these days. Fosdick draws to a close in typical forceful language:

> At any rate, for my part, I made up my mind long ago that I would never be minister of one of those churches that open their doors two or three days a week so that some one could make a speech about religion and for the rest serve no better purpose than to be decorative backgrounds for undertakers' signs.[2]

Most if not all the issues confronting preachers who share the liberal view of religion are to be found in this sermon. We shall examine these issues, drawing upon Dr. Fosdick and upon other ministers who agree with this point of view.

THE ROLE OF THE BIBLE

A central question was an understanding of the Bible. The battle over the validity of "higher criticism" raged during this period and is still very much alive today. By the late twenties, fundamentalism was being severely attacked in seminaries, churches, and indeed in the courts of law. Was the Bible to be understood literally, particularly in its explanation of the origin of human life as recorded in Genesis? In oversimplified terms, are we descended from apes or are we made by God in God's own image and likeness? Are the hypotheses of Darwin to be taken as the correct explanation of the origin of our species? If so, can religion admit that the scientific explanation of the source and cause of human life is the correct one? Does this not subject the Bible to the charge that it is not accurate and unerring in all detail? Dare one argue that there are many biblical accounts that are myths—that is, not grounded in historical fact but in some poetic description, for which the story is an imaginative, theological reflection on the meaning of life?

The initial religious root of the conflict grew in foreign soil—in German scholarship. Outstanding ministers such as Henry Sloane Coffin studied in Europe and returned convinced that the doctrine of literal or verbal inspiration of the Bible must be set aside. The Bible was not to be studied as a scientific account of our origins, but as a record of the spiritual growth and development of the life created by God. Furthermore, the biblical accounts suggested a progressive revelation to the Jews, and later to the Christians, of God's fundamental purpose and goal. There was no inherent conflict between science and religion, for each in its own way attested to the purpose of existence and in that sense shared a common faith in the future.

Fosdick's book, *The Modern Use of the Bible*, articulated this opinion.[3] It became for many a seminal expression of a way of preaching to countless numbers of people for whom the older literalistic view had caused enormous problems. The inquiring empirical methodologies of science had created something like the recent "death of God" mentality and were shaking the foundations of their received faith.

The breach between the sacred and the secular was widening. This new understanding of the Bible might well be a bridge to throw across the abyss, enabling conversation and community to develop. Countless sermons sought to establish that bridge, arguing that religion and science shared common goals, that both suggested a progressive development of life, and that on the whole this development was for the better. They suggested that God was working in the world not only through religion, but within science as well. Both religion and science, they said, point to some higher purpose, which is in some profound sense spiritual. This view was well stated by James Gordon Gilkey, minister of South Congregational Church in Springfield, Massachusetts:

> How do we picture God's activity at the beginning of things? We believe that God, working in the midst of space and time and created matter, organized it into the system of universes which science is now revealing. When our inorganic earth, a tiny part of one of the universes, reached a certain state of development, God put into it the first sparks of life. Ever since then, He has been sending more and more life into our growing world, just as the sun radiates fresh lightwaves every new instant of time.[4]

This merger of aims, something like a concordat between religion and science, resulted in sermons showing that providence and evolution were by no means in opposition. John Monroe Moore preached a sermon titled "Progress—God's Way of Deliverance and Revelation," in which he argues that the "consciousness that the movement of the race is according to a righteous purpose and an intelligent plan gives confidence to people. . . . Human development is a possibility, a tremendous possibility. That is the dominant faith of the modern era and lies at the basis of modern thought and action."[5]

Joseph Fort Newton suggests that the notion of progressive revelation—the idea of God going somewhere—tends to undergird and support the views of modern science. "Instead of a world made like a watch, wound up and set going, with which God interferes here and there, God is found to be the Life and Meaning of the universe, his will its rhythm, his purpose its reason for being."[6]

Many felt that this growing coalition between science and religion would destroy faithlessness and encourage belief in the Bible, which now could be understood and accepted by intelligent people. An interesting development was the argument that religion could be seen to be like science, in that it too used the scientific method to validate its belief claims: Religious experiences were so much data to be studied, examined, and tested; hypotheses could be shown to be true or false. Through this reasoning, it could be shown that both science and religion proceed by faith and that both discover a world of law and order. "In this way," wrote E. Y. Mullins, president of Southern Baptist Theological Seminary, "men gradually came to see that science and religion are in full agreement in their basic attitudes and instincts. Both work by faith. . . . Both learn by experience that doubt paralyzes while faith stimulates."[7]

In "Evolution and Religion," a sermon by Ernest Fremont Tittle, an outstanding Methodist preacher, it is argued that if one were to apply the evolutionary hypothesis to Jesus' words, they would become "startlingly meaningful." He then cites two instances: "My Father worketh even until now, and I work" (John 5:17 ASV); "The earth beareth fruit of itself; first the blade, then the ear, then the full grain in the ear" (Mark 4:28 ASV). As Tittle exegetes this latter text, one may agree that the phrase "My Father worketh even until now" has meaning in terms of the evolutionary hypothesis, not "in spite of the fact, but by reason of the fact that he has come to believe in evolution." One may be able to think of God "as having been continually at work in the world, causing the inorganic to become organic."[8]

The appeal of this sermon to people who shared Tittle's concerns is most evident. He sought for words and ideas that would enable people to hear the biblical message once again. Theological language trapped in the interpretations given by fundamentalists, he believed, did more to conceal than to reveal the truths about life that are needed for this new age. The ideas of progressive revelation and development and evolution provided those truths. Further- more, the evolutionary hypothesis suggested that not the past, but the present and the possibilities for the future are the proper starting point of sermons. If preaching is to be effective, it must begin where people are. This is necessary, not only because, as in all ages, people struggle with cares and problems for which religion must offer some solace but because the real issues facing people now are indeed "where the action is." The same God who worked in the past works now; revelation continues.

"Beginning where people are" now became the proper way to prepare a sermon. Dr. Fosdick called it the project method; others, the inductive approach. Fosdick believed that preachers had been straitjacketed too long by an expository method of preaching, which tended to ignore the congregation's situation. "Only the preacher," he writes, "proceeds still from the idea that folk come to church desperately anxious to discover what happened to the Jebusites."[9] He felt that the main function of the sermon is to address people's problems and concerns and to show how the text could throw light upon them. Indeed, reading Fosdick's sermons with care, one sees that this method is used again and again. A problem is stated, to which the text offers a solution. The interface between them is demonstrated through a wide-ranging appeal to examples in literature, science, psychology, and other so-called secular disciplines that attest to the truth of the religious claim in the text. All these illustrations become so much evidence to be drawn upon.

Joseph Fort Newton summarized this strategy for preaching, arguing that only an inductive approach will win the hearts and minds of people, for it is the method used in other fields of inquiry as well and is congenial to the modern temperament. "In the old days, the text was a truth assumed to be true, and the preacher only needed to expound its meaning, deduce its lessons and apply them." The task of preaching, then, was to begin with a life situation in 1933, not in Corinth in 50 A.D. Newton then proceeded to apply this approach in the sermon "You Cannot Serve Both God and Mammon." He begins with the observation that factory life produces fatigue and weariness because the mind is divided. At the theater or when playing golf one experiences a minimum of weariness because the mind is not divided—because there is a single-minded enjoyment. Why is this true? The message of the text is attested to by our own experience. We have discovered in our own daily life that we must be wholly bent upon, or directed by, one goal. Building upon this experience, which we can validate for ourselves, "the minister may now skillfully use a sense of intellectual satisfaction as an opportunity to create a deep sense of spiritual satisfaction."[10]

One is struck in such sermons by the appeal to the inherent reasonableness of religion as a genuine experience to be felt and in some sense proven. Actually, something like a science of empirical theology was developed by C.D. Macintosh, who argued that it is possible to apply scientific methods "in the realms of religious knowledge in such a way as to distinguish the data of theology from other elements of experience." The underlying assumption justifying this investigation was that the "divine reality" is dependable, just as the scientist in his inquiries assumes the dependability of nature. Furthermore, progress toward the "right religious adjustment" results in certain experiences that carry the force of truth. These were said to be the development of good character, "a sensitiveness to sin, the peace of reconciliation, and unselfish love to God and man."[11]

The final force of this "philosophical" argument was that the truth claims of religion are validated by the moral fruits they produce. Charles R. Brown states, "It was the Master of all the higher values in life who proposed this pragmatic test, the test of experience, the ability or the inability of the thing under scrutiny to work out *satisfactory* results."[12] He goes on to argue that as we test the truth claims of all other branches of life—music, art, literature—we must let religion stand or fall in the same manner.

THE HUMANITY OF JESUS

The acceptance of the evolutionary hypothesis led to an essential theological principle that shaped the sermons of many preachers. It went something like this: Evolution suggests the growth and development of life—all life, of both simple and complex organisms—the final fruit of which is human nature. The Bible tells us that God is the ultimate creator of this process; thus it can be argued that the intention of all creation is, in the deepest sense, good. For at the heart of things there is a "living, loving God." This loving God has initiated a "vast growth process." Thus there is a divine intention unfolding, growing, developing, which moves towards the perfection of personality. The full expression of what we are meant to become, and in a sense implicitly already are, is shown to us in the person of Jesus, who is the embodiment of the potentiality inherent in us all. We are destined to become sons and daughters of a God who is the Father of all races.

Acceptance of this view of progressive revelation and of its assurance of final victory encouraged a deeply felt optimistic attitude toward life, in spite of all the problems of daily existence. One could argue that, while the past also was surely a time of divine disclosures, these revelations were less clear to people living then; they saw through a glass darkly. God has still more to reveal in our era—a time of new revelation. Religion then "relates to the best ideals in the souls of men. . . . They are the shadows of God in the human mind," as one preacher put it. What we are to become is already latent in us and unfolds much as the web grows from the spider. It was not said that such development is inevitable, for as history shows, we are capable of enormous evil. What was being maintained is that we are capable of higher development and that what we do or what we become is a decision we can and must make. We are capable of sinning, but we are capable also of magnificent deeds of love and justice. Thus, while the final form of the future lies in God's hands, "he has no other hands than ours to do his will today."

The main purpose of preachers of that era was to clarify the understanding of the real identity of Jesus. His essential nature and purpose, long obscured by complex creedal statements, are those of the prophet who fulfills, in his life, ministry, and death, the great expectations predicted in the Old Testament. Formulations of Jesus' nature expressed in creeds are not necessarily false, but rather are expressions of faith developed in the language and thought-forms of another age. As Dr. Herbert Lockwood Willett of the University of Chicago expressed it, "the atonement must now be conceived of as a plain, human task, undertaken by Jesus as the representative of humanity, and not achieved by him in a mysterious transcendental way. . . . To speak of Jesus in terms which imply his Godhead is merely to confuse terms and set obstacles before simple and trusting faith."[13] Willett is not arguing that Jesus, in some fashion, must be fundamentally differentiated from God. He is saying that the titles ascribed to Jesus; the endless attempts to clarify the meaning of the statement that he is the Christ—to unravel the human and divine characteristics of his nature—boggle the contemporary mind. "He is," continues Willett, "the son of God, but he is even more than this—the son of man. . . . It is the title he loved, and by which he named himself."

Preachers of the liberal tradition did not hesitate to clothe Jesus in contemporary terms to make him more available to their congregations and to make religion more meaningful. This understandable wish resulted more in making Jesus like we are than in making us like he is. Thus Jesus was called an optimist, whose confidence in the "human race is one of his peculiar marks of divinity." One preacher observed that Jesus "believed in our ability to discern moral issues . . . in our ability to fight our way out of evil and into the presence of God."[14]

In a sermon entitled "The Mind of Christ," Raymond Calkins asked rhetorically, What characterizes the mind of Christ? His answer revealed as much about his evaluation of Christian attitudes as it did about the mind of Christ. Christ's mind is independent, he said, and unconventional. It is above local and racial prejudice. He is a nonconformist, capable of independent thinking. Christ's mind "outlaws a selfish and egotistical and narrow nationalism, and declares for cooperation, brotherhood, and mutual service in international relations."[15] Another preacher called Jesus of Nazareth "the greatest of all radicals," who by both precept and example disclosed the true moral life. He was, as well, a teacher and leader who evokes from us the best that we are. In fact, "The religion of Jesus is a religion of heroes."[16]

Sometimes the boundless enthusiasm of these preachers found expression in images that strained and cracked—images too limited to contain the dynamism they sought to express. Thus, even a preacher as well known as Ralph W. Sockman could fall into this error. "Jesus did not coach his immortal squad, the world's most famous eleven, by merely urging them to increased effort of will. No good coach contents himself with mere urging. He feeds the imaginations of his squad with ideas of success. He develops in them a winning spirit."[17]

By carefully comparing the teachings and the healing ministry of Jesus with the findings of psychology, preachers were led to discover that Jesus was, among other things, the first psychologist, or at least that his healings were being confirmed more and more in that newly developing science. Even the language of psychology was drawn upon to illustrate this essential connection. "Jesus' method," as Albert Parker Fitch conceived it, "was not negative and repressive. He sought to release men from repression and enable forces of higher development to grow." He then illustrated this principle by describing the manner in which Jesus called Peter, James, and John to be his disciples.[18] Rather than addressing them as persons who were performing menial tasks, he saw their latent possibilities. He evoked the best in them, as expressed through their occupation: "Come after me and I will make you fishers of men."

In all these citations, the emphasis has been upon the tremendous possibilities latent in human nature. One famous liberal preacher, Washington Gladden, delivered a series of lectures at the First Congregational Church, Columbus, Ohio, in which he set forth a theology for preaching and for social action. He argued that we now see more clearly "that God is our Father and that we are his children." From this initial premise he drew the conclusion that children must then be of the same nature as their father. Therefore "everything that is essentially human is included in the nature of God; everything that is essentially divine is found in the nature of man." It thus follows that there is no inherent contradiction between our nature and his. Accepting this premise, then, we have rid ourselves of the dualism that "insists upon putting humanity and deity into two separate categories. And Jesus Christ stands forth not only as the rightness of the Father's glory, but as the perfect flower of humanity."[19]

It was furthermore maintained that Jesus, the Son of God, and at the same time "the perfect flower of humanity," was the full and complete expression in history of the eternal truths and values that ennoble life and toward which all life moves. These liberal preachers shared the conviction that, with the coming of Christ, the civilizing truths about human nature that are taught in a classical education are not to be discarded as profane, but rather, in their own way, point to him. Thus it was that the standard method of exegeting texts was to discover their moral truths that illustrate eternal principles. Albert Parker Fitch maintained that the moral and spiritual values that matter were not invented by Jesus—"He only discovered them." His authority for this was Lessing, the German philosopher. Ernest Fremont Tittle argued that people desire good, not evil; beauty, not ugliness. He went on, "But when men climb to a higher plane where truth and beauty and goodness stand out clear and compelling . . . they know that Tennyson spoke truly when, summing up his personal faith, he said, 'There's something that watches over us all and our individuality endures.' "[20]

In the Lyman Beecher Lectures on Preaching in 1942, Dr. Sockman reaffirmed the basic conviction that moral values are eternal and that Jesus is the exponent and example of true values. Lyrically, he sang the praises of truth, beauty, and goodness. "Truth crushed to the earth will rise again. . . .Beauty survives brutality. Artists will paint tomorrow. Poets will sing tomorrow. . . . And as for goodness, it does seem that about everything the world's Best Man stood for is being challenged. But the Black Friday on which he was crucified became the Good Friday of history."[21]

This faith in the human potential for good, urged and motivated by the supreme example of Jesus, the pioneer and author of faith, provided a bouyancy and vigor for attacking social issues. The creed of the liberals included as a central element the belief in the future dawning of the kingdom of God on earth. Preachers did develop sermons concerned with resurrection and often preached on the theme of immortality; their primary emphasis, however, dealt with the historical realization of Jesus' teachings about a new world order, in which justice and love would shape social and political life on this planet. In their enthusiasm and zeal for social justice and their belief in the theology they preached, some tended to play down or overlook the fact that the human potential for good was all too clearly balanced by the potential for evil. Something like the first flush of dawn colored their sermons as they saw a new age and a hopeful future before them. The past and its heritage of suffering finally would be overcome, they believed, and religion would play a central role in the attainment of that new world.

The sermons of Fosdick and others who shared his theological interpretation of the times were balanced and insightful, but sometimes grim. It is to Fosdick's everlasting credit that he was one of the first preachers of this age who saw the evils of prejudice, particularly against blacks, named it for what it was, and used the sermon as a means of denouncing the real failings of American society.

> It is not merely our personal whim and fancy that we do not like Japanese, Jews, Italians, Negroes or what you will. All such lumping of masses of God's children in one group, and cherishing prejudice and dislike against them is our share in the most powerful enemy that Christianity faces today—the racial-national philosophy.[22]

This was written just at the onset of the Second World War and accurately described prevailing American attitudes toward minorities. It was not only accurate but courageous, and typical of Fosdick. He had addressed the League of Nations in Geneva, setting forth his lifelong belief in pacifism, even as the United States Senate was voting against this nation's participation in the League. His own personal ordeal may be traced in sermons preached during World War II, when it became evident that to fight against the tyranny of Nazis was vital, but not the ideal of the gospel. Thus, while he did not deny the necessity of that war, he never ceased to warn his congregation at Riverside Church in New York City that the evils of the Nazi philosophy were latent in all people, including Americans. This he preached when American patriotism and the belief in the essential goodness of this nation was at its height.

Nor was Fosdick alone in the struggle for social justice. During the height of the Great Depression, Roy L. Smith argued that that national catastrophe was traceable in a large part to the nation's refusal to accept moral laws as taught by Jesus. He described that era as a time of death for the gods of rugged individualism, prosperity, and money. Those gods had promised ease and abundance but had produced instead the loss of all the nation's resources and had created breadlines. He argued that "because the law of cause and effect is inviolable, we must rest assured that our present dilemma is a direct result of defiance of some moral law by which the world is ruled."[23] Ernest Fremont Tittle preached a sermon entitled "Bread of God" during this same period, warning Americans that the nation could not have bread as its god and at the same time practice racial exclusion against Asians. He attacked excessive tariffs on imports from Europe, and the United States Chamber of Commerce, for sponsoring them.

In all this, one is aware that the liberals saw the passionate commitment to social and political change as the proper business of religion. Liberal theology offered a way to understand oneself as a child of God, the Father of us all, who is calling all people to enter into a brotherhood. It not only offered an inner sense of identity, but provided the impetus to change society. Preachers such as Fosdick would challenge members of their congregations to put the teachings of Jesus into practice by altering social conditions in the marketplace. If they really believed in Jesus, they would do works such as his. Religion was not to be understood primarily as a private matter, dealing with a person's inner secret life with God; it was, as well, the obligation to change the world, where one had influence and could do so.

No one better expressed the dominant hope of this era than did Henry Sloane Coffin, who said in the sermon "The Realism of Faith,"

[in] the after-look of history our generation may prove a revealing period when the Sun of Righteousness rose with healing in His wings and some of the world's sorest ills were done away with—self-centered nationalism, ruthless competition, neglect of the human beings who

create wealth, above all neglect of the spirit of brotherhood in industry, in politics, in international relations. Yes, a creative period when spiritual riches came into being.[24]

AN APPRAISAL

Looking back upon the so-called liberal era in America, which roughly spanned the period between the two world wars, it is easy to trace the needs that evoked its appearance, as well as the errors it made. We who live now in a period of disillusionment, suffering from what has been called a failure of nerve, or a loss of identity, yearn perhaps nostalgically for the assurance and élan that those preachers so clearly felt and proclaimed. They developed an understanding of the Bible that enabled them to proclaim religion as a viable option in a complex, depressed, and confused world. They "de-divinized" Jesus, having discerned in his teachings and life a program for action. They cast themselves into the worldly arena, using the pulpit as a vehicle for social protest. They encouraged ecumenical discussion among the major denominations, hoping to ally all Christians of whatever stripe in some common declaration of faith, which would enable them all to share together in correcting social evils. They created a language—the common speech of daily life—as the vehicle for sermons. They appealed to the reason and conscience, calling upon people to recognize how much religion really mattered in their lives and in the future of society. They felt that democracy, as enunciated in the American experiment, foreshadowed the great ideals of justice as taught by Jesus. They believed that people could practice what was preached. In short, they provided a faith for hard times.

It is vital to realize that hope for the end of all wars, proclaimed following the First World War, and the promise of a dawning age of democracy had been ruined by the Great Depression and the onset of World War II. Rather than retreating from the world and consigning its future to inevitable destruction, or turning their thoughts to a future life beyond the grave, they cast themselves into the fray, insisting that life here and now is the scene of action in which to find God and to create a new world order. Theirs was a theology of hope.

Be that as it may, the first critique of liberal theology and of the ministers who proclaimed it from their pulpits came from chastened liberals, at the beginning of the Second World War. It seemed that all their dreams for the future had been shattered and their inevitable reaction was disappointment. Deeper still, a sense of hopelessness had arisen. Reinhold Niebuhr wrote a book during the 30s, significantly titled *Reflections at the End of an Era*. He predicted that the theology that dreamed of a world "lapt in universal Law," a quotation from Tennyson's *Locksley Hall*, would soon collapse. Another of Niebuhr's books, *Leaves from the Notebooks of a Tamed Cynic*, which should be required reading for all in the church who want to become involved in politics, contained one essential criticism of ministers—naiveté in the political and social arena.

> One of the most fruitful sources of self-deception in the ministry is the proclamation of great ideals and principles without any clue to their relation to the controversial issues of the day. . . . I wish that some of our romanticists and sentimentalists could sit through a series of meetings where the real social problems of a city were discussed.[25]

He charged that political innocence was shaped by an overly optimistic belief in human nature—something like the assumption that if people knew the truth, they would act on it. If religion were reasonable—if its program for life offered the possibility of a just society—would people not throw themselves gladly into the struggle?

Fosdick himself, in later years, strongly attacked this charge, arguing that while some ministers may have exhibited an overly optimistic belief in the potential of human nature, the mainstream of preaching and social action was far more sober. Most did not, he argued, share in or believe in the view that progress was inevitable or automatic.

Certainly the tendency to read the Bible as a history of the progressive revelation of God's will for the world must be sharply attacked. It is also now seen that the inclination to regard Jesus as the Son of man, and ourselves as his spiritual sons and daughters, is a reading of the New Testament that must be questioned. The liberals were people shaped by their ethos. Their religious beliefs did not spring up out of religious reflection on the Bible alone; they were formed by the people's own cultural and even their national beliefs. Nevertheless, what they stood for still lives and challenges us today. They felt that history is the place where Christians must act out their beliefs; that religion is not what a person does in his or her solitude. They also had faith in the future—the future as envisioned by their dream of the kingdom of God on earth. We are deeply in their debt. And, if we fault their views, then we must fashion our own theology for this era.

IV. FUNDAMENTALISM:
THE EVANGELISTS

Jesus Saves, Jesus Saves

Both in the sermons of Paul Tillich and in those of the liberals, certain assumptions are shared. One of these is the recognition that a credibility gap exists and is widening, separating the traditional statements of the Christian faith from the intellectual climate of this age. Another is the realization, growing out of this assumption, that a revision of religious language is of paramount importance if people are to become aware of the vitality of the Christian faith and of its essential importance to life. Both forms of preaching affirm the necessity to relate Christian faith to modern thought and to consciously make use of metaphors and images growing out of the so-called nonreligious disciplines, in order to clarify what faith affirms. They see this ongoing contact and resultant dialogue as essential for preaching.

It is necessary at this point, however, to observe that there is a preaching tradition very much alive and growing that does not share these assumptions nor the conclusions developed from them. I refer to evangelistic preaching, whose most prominent and successful exponent is Billy Graham.[1] Almost single-handedly, he has succeeded in evoking something like a spiritual revival among Protestants and Catholics alike. Churches that share his understanding of the nature and purpose of preaching flourish, while so-called liberal churches are experiencing a decline in both membership and money. It is common enough to hear the argument set forth that evangelistic preaching reflects a frontier age; that it is anti-intellectual; that it is purely emotional; that it has no lasting effect; and that it is basically sectarian, resulting in no substantial change in culture.

In my judgment, however, we would do well to come to some serious understanding of a positive and sympathetic nature as to what a sermon in this tradition intends, how it is developed, and what presuppositions inform its structure. We may see that something like a typology is possible, because while fundamentalists come in many shapes and sizes, and are often at odds with one another, they share a common allegiance when it comes to a theology of preaching. Let us then look at evangelistic preaching, drawing notably upon Dr. Graham, but upon others as well.

THE CENTRALITY OF THE BIBLE

The subject matter for such preaching is the gospel of Jesus Christ as proclaimed in the Bible by the apostles, as predicted by the prophets, and as authenticated by Jesus Christ himself. There is no other authority for preaching; no other subject matter; no source material other than this one Book, which is the absolute norm and standard for all preaching. When Dr. Graham proclaims dramatically, with the Book held aloft, "The Bible says," he certainly is not consciously striking a media-drenched pose. "Insincerity" is the easiest, least provable response, but is an accusation that can be leveled equally well against those who make it. No, the point Dr. Graham is dramatizing is that for him, the Bible is the beginning and end of prayerful reflection, out of which the sermon grows. This seems obvious and is so often repeated that it almost has lost significance, but it needs repetition. Preaching, for the evangelists, begins with God's disclosure to preachers—his Word—divinely inspired and revealed only in the Scriptures. This Book sets forth the subject matter of the sermon, the form it is to take, the people to whom it is to be addressed, and the ultimate purpose of the sermon itself. Look, for example, at Dr. Graham's sermon "Heaven and Hell," delivered in Madison Square Garden. This sermon develops a variety of arguments to support his conviction that there is a heaven. That conviction is based solely upon his reading of the Bible, and the logic of the sermon follows from his reading. "I personally believe," he says, "that the Bible teaches that Heaven is going to be our home."[2]

Since the Bible teaches this, the development of the sermon demonstrates how contemporary scientific thought affirms the truth stated in the Bible. This is the fundamentalist point of view, characteristic of this form of preaching, and needs to be noted from the beginning. The authority for spiritual and moral concerns may be drawn only from the Bible, and this form of logic holds true as well for scientific or philosophical speculations as to our nature and destiny. Thus Graham asks himself where heaven might be located. The issue is not, Is there a literal heaven of which the Bible speaks? but How might one imagine heaven in terms of biblical imagery, even in the light of our present scientific understanding of the universe?

> Scientists tell us there are a hundred million stars in our galaxy. Now we don't measure distance in miles. We measure it in light years. With light traveling at the rate of 186,000 miles per second, eleven million miles per minute, the sun is only eight light minutes from us. One light year is six trillion miles. Our galaxy, just our galaxy, is one hundred thousand light years in diameter. There are one hundred thousand million stars and planets. I believe that out there somewhere God can find some place to put us in heaven.[3]

The argument is clear enough. If there is a heaven, understood or imagined in some localized sense, contemporary science in its discoveries about the nature of the universe by no means disproves it. If anything, recent discoveries in astronomy may make it more conceivable. "The Bible says that the morning stars all sing together. Scientists said, 'No.' Now they know the heavenly bodies literally give off phonetic vibrations. The morning stars *do* sing together. Science was wrong—the Bible was right!"[4] The appeal of such arguments is to our reason; it is deductive, not inductive. One does not begin with speculations about the nature of the universe in order to arrive at a conclusion, which then finds support in biblical statements. Just the reverse is true! It is the declarations of the Bible that give guidance to our anxieties about the apparent infinitude of space and time. Far from frightening us and diminishing our faith, the infinite spaces suggest the probability of heaven's location there as a conceivable thought.

The argument from the authority of the Bible is a standard position of evangelists and is supported in a variety of ways. One of these is the simple observation that there must be some recognized authority in matters of religion. Just as science and other disciplines have their canons, so does religion. Without these, one is given over to a plurality of conflicting authorities, with no way of evaluation other than through private opinion. Thus people are cast into the abyss of subjectivism with its corresponding loss of certainty. In order to be delivered from this confusion, people must recognize one ultimate court of appeal, and that is the Bible. "Here is the dictated Word of God, inerrant, without fault, without flaw, without variableness, without shadow as though of turning. . . . We do not have to investigate its pages, weigh them, measure them, mirror them, analyse them, balance them, to see if there be found any flaw in them."[5]

While these preachers do not "analyse" the pages to see "if there be found any flaw in them," they do study them assiduously and discover that the Bible is self-authenticating. One proof of this is the argument from prophecy. V. P. Black, an evangelist, argues that the "prophets could never have manipulated prophecy to cover so accurately and in such detail the virgin birth, the vicarious suffering and death, the blood atonement, and the resurrection of the Son of Man. Such manipulation is not humanly possible!" Since these prophets lived "hundreds of years before Christ was born" and since their prophecies were completely fulfilled, their testimony "would be sufficient to convince any rational person that Jesus Christ is everything he claimed to be."[6]

A number of ancillary beliefs are contained in sermons of this tradition. One is the conviction that in the Bible we are dealing with actual persons, dates, locations, and events—not with myths, fables, or legends about people who in fact did not exist. Hence Black's conviction as to the integrity of the prophetic witness. How may one doubt the truthfulness of the claim of people who were inspired by the same God whose final revelation is in Jesus Christ?

Granting these assumptions, the arguments developed are highly rational and are calculated to appeal to the mind of the hearer.

When it is granted that the Bible does not err, and does in fact set forth a plan for salvation for all people, then a basic form of logic common to this type of preaching is developed: the either/or logic. In more dramatic form it might be called the two-roads logic.

> Jesus Christ taught us that there are two roads of life. He taught that there are two masters. You are either mastered by self or you are mastered by God, and he said you cannot serve both at the same time. . . . And he said that there are two destinies, heaven and hell. Now Christ does not divide men into Black and White, or rich or poor. . . . He divides us into two classes—those who are on the broad road that leads to destruction and those on the narrow road that leads to eternal life. Which road are you on?[7]

The reasoning of the argument is inescapable, and the choice appears to be genuine, assuming that the Bible is taken to be the supreme authority for both minister and congregation. The function of this sermon is to make that choice abundantly clear. Indeed, its primary purpose is to call upon people to decide a matter of life and death. The sermon, then, is a means of judgment and grace. It is, in fact, God speaking through the preacher to the people, who are moved by the Holy Spirit.

Another theological assumption based upon this understanding of the place of the Bible in religious life is the conviction that Jesus Christ is the same yesterday, today, and tomorrow. The movement of faith and reflection is not from the past forward, but from the present backward. This argument is not the same as the one in which we actually interpret the past in terms of our present situation. Rather, it assumes that although civilizations and cultures have undergone change since the first century A.D., people have not. Our needs, temptations, desires, and goals remain the same. That being granted, we can and must project ourselves backward, imagining ourselves to be there among the crowds who followed Jesus—among those who believed and those who jeered as he was being crucified. The hymn containing the line "Were you there when they crucified my Lord?" is a standard in this tradition.

Thus realistic descriptions of biblical accounts, including customs, traditions, dress, and even dramatic narratives between biblical characters, assume a realistic, contemporary meaning. One has only to note the art portraying that era and to observe the violent reaction when biblical scenes are cast in a modern situation, with Jesus clothed in contemporary costume. Furthermore, the behavior of the prophets, the disciples, and the other people in the biblical accounts is alive and contemporary behavior from which we may draw lessons for our lives.

This movement backward in time to the source is necessary because the Bible teaches that God's final revelation was given once and for all in Jesus Christ. Therefore all succeeding religious thought and teaching has been and will be but a development of that fundamental treasury of prophecy and fulfillment. One must always return to the past, for there lies the truth as an infallible standard by which to measure all subsequent traditions of religious thought and life. Thus, while the sermon certainly deals with the present situation, the explanation of our human condition is not located in the present but in the past. Therefore a conscious effort is made, as it were, to relive the past. "To walk where Jesus walked" is far more than the wish of an archaeologist; it is the hope of people for whom history—their real history—has been located. There lies my true history! There lived the persons whose behavior I must emulate! There are given the rules and guides for preparing for the future!

But for what reason is this kind of sermon developed? What is the fundamental purpose that shapes it? It is to offer the hearer the possibility of eternal life in Jesus Christ. "I want to talk tonight about the future life and the choice we must make now," says Billy Graham. It is neither an exaggeration nor a "put down" to say that this is the theme of all his sermons, regardless of the text. It is, furthermore, the overriding concern of every sermon in this tradition. It is the conviction of these preachers that the Bible has to do with one subject alone: God's promise of a future life and joy in heaven for those who are obedient, as well as the corresponding assurance that those who do not hear this promise, and those who turn their backs upon it, are going to hell. Hence the urgent tone for the right decision now. In a sermon dealing with the resurrection, Dr. Black concludes his arguments with this emotional plea:

> My sinner friends, I plead for you to come while we sing the invitation. Paul said, "Today if you hear my voice harden not your hearts." Tomorrow is the philosophy of fools, that day you may never have. . . . I am pleading with you tonight to turn away from the world that will cheat you; from Satan who will destroy you; and come to Christ who will save you. The clock says today; the calendar says today; the sickbed says so; that trainwreck says today . . . your heart-beat says today.[8]

The passionate concern heard in these lines is the basic topic shared by all evangelists. Saving souls is their business, God's business, and the reason for preaching. The Bible teaches that this world is a "vale of soul-making." In all details, it points to the future, not the present, as the time and place of ultimate importance. The present is the time for decision; people here and now must choose how they will live in the eternal life after death. The function of the past is to show us, through revelation in the words of the Bible, where we now stand and what tomorrow's prospects may be. In one sense then, people do decide what their future is to be. For although God's plan for all life has already been, as it were, enacted in Jesus Christ, we still have the chance to decide for it or against it. The future is not simply an open possibility to be created by us. Its contours and directions are given. Therefore one may look forward into tomorrow with genuine confidence because of the promises given by God. This is a theology of hope that is rational, makes sense, and has some order and clarity. As one evangelist pointed out, "Frankly, I think it's pretty smart not to want to go to hell. I think it's one of the smartest decisions you will ever make in your life. I know that to be saved is to have heaven on earth. It means you'll go to heaven when you die."[9]

This way of understanding our nature and destiny shapes the ethical dimensions of the sermon. It is often said that evangelistic preaching is not concerned with social justice, or with the need to change society so that it may be more in conformity with the teachings of Jesus. One must remember, however, the understanding of the human situation that dominates this preaching. In the first place, the contention is that preaching about morality and social change has proven to be a dismal failure. As William Ward Ayer puts it, "For the last quarter of a century the Church has been preaching morals, and immorality is on the increase."[10] Second, the strategy of such preaching is not designed to change society. That society needs change because it is in the grip of Satan is, of course, affirmed. The first priority, however, is a fundamental change in individuals. If persons are not saved, they are in the hands of Satan and cannot perform good works; their intentions are evil, and they are bound to do works of evil. Finally, however, the evangelists' paramount purpose is to save souls. To be lost, to roam through life without Christ, to face a future life in hell is the worst of all possible conditions. "Think of what it must be to lose one's soul, to be lost forever without the center of one's existence, namely, Christ, to be wandering without rest. That is the ultimate reward, the final tragedy of iniquity."[11]

This attitude toward the world, society, and social change is a complex affair. Evangelists are concerned with both personal and social relations, for the world is called upon to obey the teachings of Jesus. However, their understanding of what is possible and what is demanded is shaped by their doctrine of human nature and by their belief about the future. There are moral laws just as precise, clear, and inevitable as the laws operating in the natural world. "As good citizens," says Billy Graham, "we ought to help every good project in our community. As good citizens we ought to do what we can to make this a better place in which to live." At the same time, as pressing and demanding as these obligations are for the Christian, one's real and ultimate consideration is the present state of one's soul, in terms of one's real future. Our life span is at best seventy years or so, and beyond stretches an eternity. Indeed, the Bible teaches that we have no permanent resting place here, for we are a colony of heaven—heaven is our real home. While speculation as to what heaven is like can never be more than an imaginative construction drawn from the biblical promises, it is at least "the utopia that we have dreamed of and thought that maybe we could build on this earth, and have failed."[12]

In the sermon on heaven and hell, to which a number of references have been made, Graham suggests that in heaven there will be no racial discrimination, no poverty, no war, and "the policeman won't have anything to do." The Christian attitude toward a neighbor is certainly of fundamental importance, for not everyone who cries, "Lord, Lord, will enter the kingdom of Heaven." Graham has taken many positive steps through his crusades to attack racial discrimination. He obviously seeks to build bridges of understanding between the races. At the same time, he does not consider this to be his primary function as a preacher. The purpose of this sermon, as we have previously stated, is to win souls for Christ and at the close it leads to an invitation in the form of an altar call. People are invited—urged—to confess or to testify or to reaffirm their decision to accept Christ. Furthermore, the call to come forward is issued in dramatic terms, designed to heighten the sense of urgency, for a battle between Satan and God rages in our hearts. Only Christ and his atoning sacrifice on the cross offer us the blessed assurance of victory in this contest and the certainty of eternal life.

THE NEED OF THE PEOPLE

Evangelists make certain assumptions about the nature of the congregations to whom they preach, based upon their reading of the Bible. The first of these is the conviction, as we have seen, that people stand in need of salvation. The second is that the people know this, and that they attend evangelical services with anxious and hopeful hearts. Says Graham, "Whatever the color of the skin, or whatever the accent we speak, our hearts are the same—the same fears, the same longings, the same sins—troubles, problems, difficulties. Well, I tell you tonight Christ can help you."[13] It is assumed that all people can understand the message to be offered and that all desire to hear it. In the tradition of missionary preaching of the nineteenth century, the evangelist feels compelled by the gospel to reach all humankind, for it is through hearing the saving word that souls are redeemed from sin, Satan, and hell. This means there must be a given sphere of discourse between preacher and congregation, and that sphere is the language of the texts. It may be useful at times to draw upon contemporary sociological or psychological data to illustrate the evils of the age, but all such references are used only to support the truth of the Bible's view of our human condition; they do not prove anything in and of themselves. The message about Jesus Christ is self-authenticating; it carries its own interpretation to the hungry hearts of those who hear it and know that they are being addressed.

Because this is so, the so-called crisis of religious language, which afflicts the other traditions of preaching dealt with in this book, is not felt by evangelists. The biblical language about heaven, hell, Satan, sin, and judgment is understood as needing no translation or accommodation to contemporary views of the universe, its origin, and its future. If anything, a serious examination of contemporary culture discloses to a perceptive person the accuracy of the biblical description of life as we know it. Graham observes, for example, that one seldom hears a sermon about hell, and yet everybody uses the word. He then goes on to describe a recent conversation with a psychiatrist who had observed that the fear of going to hell is, in some way, deeply imbedded in the subconscious. Evangelists believe that the language of the Bible accurately describes our real situation and provides the contextual situation in which the offer of heaven and eternal life needs to be proclaimed. This being the case, it is necessary only to repeat the language of the Bible, and to this end the evangelist indulges in proof texts. Rather than attempting to water down such language by assigning to it some symbolic meaning, the preacher insists upon the literal meaning. Indeed, far from seeking to diminish the threatening and sometimes lurid expressions that describe hell, its horrors are deliberately magnified.

> The thirsty will still thirst. Those who lust will still lust. The adulterer will burn with passion. The whoremonger will still rage as his blood races with the wind. The drunken will still crave drinks; the dope addict will still crave his dope; but in hell their desires will be magnified and

intensified a million fold in their intensity. It is a place of unsatisfied
passions, it's a place of no exit, it is a place of endlessness. It is a place of
unanswered prayers.[14]

Granting that the quotation just used may be called lurid—perhaps even frightening—it would nevertheless be a mistake to argue
that evangelistic sermons appeal only to the emotions of the
congregation, playing primarily upon feelings of guilt and fear of
judgment. Unquestionably, in many cases they do, but not so
much in order to create those feelings as to recognize them for what
they are and bring them into the open. It is the charlatan who seeks
to use people. In the best tradition of evangelism, such is neither
the desire nor the intention of the preachers. Rather, they wish to
set forth and demonstrate the reasonableness of the biblical
message to the people in the congregation who, it is believed, both
wish to hear this message and need to hear it for their own salvation.
A kind of catharsis is at work, in which, through the sermon and
through the preacher who delivers it, the demons are exorcised and
the people experience profound relief.

This last observation touches upon another vital point that enables
communication to take place—the passionate conviction of the
preachers, who believe themselves to be caught up in the Spirit of
God. In the tradition of the prophet, the preachers believe that God
has put words into their mouths. The preachers are convinced that
they have been saved and will often testify to life before and after
Christ came into their hearts, telling how this basically has changed
their lives. Such testimony is a powerful illustration of the power of
the gospel and cannot help but lend authenticity to the message. The
minister and the message are blended in the minds and hearts of the
people, so that often one might say that the medium is the message.
The response of the congregation itself also lends authenticity to what
has been said. When people flock to the altar, sign decision cards, or
simply attend such meetings in large numbers, they tend to
demonstrate the power of the sermon influenced by the Holy Spirit,
as channeled through the preacher and felt in the hearts of those who
listen.

Clearly such public demonstrations lend themselves all too

easily to a kind of numbers game. Sides are drawn up. Some argue that evangelistic services have no lasting effect; others argue that they do. Both appeal to numbers. Some criticize the alleged superficiality of such conversions; others testify to a new life in Christ, thanks to such preaching.[15] I doubt very much if the debaters on either side are convinced by the arguments of their opponents. One fact seems clear enough: Evangelistic preaching meets fundamental needs and is clearly on the rise in America today.

AN APPRAISAL

Granting the obvious appeal of such preaching, some questions must be asked: Why are people attracted in such large numbers? Why do evangelistic revival services fill huge auditoriums and sports stadiums all over the world? We have stated thus far the biblical reasons set forth by the preachers themselves; now we must make some assessment of the cultural situation to which they speak, and this will give us some clue as to the fundamental needs evangelists meet and apparently, fill.

It seems clear to me that such preaching, above all, offers certainty in an age of uncertainty—an Age of Anxiety. To paraphrase Paul Tillich, the sermons of this genre offer the assurance of meaning in a meaningless, frightening world. Life is said to have a definite purpose and goal that are undeniable, have existed from the beginning of time, and are set forth in God's plan. To confess Jesus Christ as one's Lord and Master is to participate in this plan and to usher in a life of peace and joy. In our particular age, the loss of the alleged purpose of American life is being proclaimed everywhere. The myths that shaped and motivated the nation's self-understanding, up to the era of the black/white confrontation and the war in Vietnam, have increasingly lost their ability to explain life, and thus in some sense, their ability to confer wholeness upon it. Such myths of course did not explain everything—no symbolic discourse does—but they did offer hope and a genuine sense of destiny, which enlarged life and described a meaningful future. These myths centered in a middle-class, white

Protestant ethic, in a nonpluralistic society, and took on a form of patriotism, expressed in the vision of America as the New Israel. Now all these assumptions have been radically challenged by events during the 1960s and 1970s. It is significant to recognize that many evangelistic preachers share this myth, consider it part of their function to evoke it in sermons, and seek to return to it as an adequate description of this nation's destiny under God.

It has been a source of concern for many critics of evangelistic preaching to observe the apparent contradiction between the religious goals and the attitude toward nation and flag. On the one hand, the logical conclusion of evangelistic preaching is a denial of the values of this world—the tendency to equate it with the world of Satan. On the other hand, many such preachers are superpatriots, who argue that the basic threat to the American way of life is Communism. They assert that Communism threatens to undermine both the religious and the social fabric of the nation. This position is maintained although the religious logic of their sermons should result in a more determined withdrawal from society and its evils, for ultimately, life as lived out here is simply a preparation for eternal life. One suspects, however, that it is just this oversimplified explanation of the source of the nation's dis-ease that attracts baffled and confused people; it is a source of relief and guidance to be confronted with a religious certainty that finds its roots in biblical affirmations, is said to be permanent and unchanging, and is a dependable guide for conduct. A correlative point, which complements and supports this conviction of certainty, is the image of authority.

We touched on this subject earlier when referring to a sermon by V. P. Black, in which he argues that people need authority in order to achieve some sense of stability. Fundamentalism's authority for faith is found within itself and nowhere else. Its claims are said to be definitively and clearly set forth in the Bible; they do not rest upon the shifting sands of science, sociology, psychology, or other human endeavors.

We thus have a kind of religious positivism that is both difficult to refute and all too easy to accept, for we are offered facts that have the force of empirical statements concerning God's dealings with people.

The way in which this is worked out in sermons is clear enough. Billy Graham offers his congregation the hope of heaven—indeed, the assurance of it. He then considers the case of a hypothetical person who desires to go to heaven but does not want to accept Jesus.

> Well, I am sorry, but I cannot compromise at that point. I have to go by the rule book. I cannot bargain. I have no authority from the Bible to bargain with your soul. I have no authority to lower the standards. Jesus said, "I am the door. By me, if any man enter in he will be saved."[16]

The point is clear. The Bible's authority sets limits and conditions with which one cannot compromise, or "bargain," as Graham says. To many people, this would seem to be a rigid, authoritarian claim that would straitjacket personal thought and decision. For others, however, just the reverse is experienced. If a religious claim is deemed to be true, and if that claim includes certain behavior demanded of those who subscribe to it, then it must come as a distinct relief to be confronted by such a clear-cut authority. There is a way leading to eternal life and a way leading to destruction. Both are clearly marked, and the pilgrim's progress is measured by the willingness to follow those markings faithfully.

On the other hand, to be told with absolute certainty that there is a plan of salvation and then to be assured that one does not have to obey certain prescribed rules in order to achieve that goal, would be tantamount to a denial of the authority of religious claims. It would likewise suggest a kind of permissiveness, which in itself is seen by many people today as a threat to the moral values claimed to be essential for both public and religious life. Indeed, the credibility of evangelists is found as much in their consistency and the logic of their requirements as in the beliefs they proclaim about the nature of existence.

Certainty, and the authority that supports it, is followed by another fundamental theme—blessed assurance. The believer who confesses his sins and accepts Jesus Christ as personal savior, need not fear the future. The often quoted existential question, Who am I? is answered in the promise of God in Jesus Christ. "Listen," says Billy Graham. "We Christians don't have to go around with our shoulders bent and discouraged and despondent. We are on our way to Heaven. This is not our home, and this is not our world. We are going to help all we can, but we are on our way to a better world."[17]

The decision to accept Christ, offered through the sermon and empowered by the Holy Spirit, results in a state of grace. One becomes a "new being," to use Tillich's terminology. Conversion results in a new personality. Furthermore, a new fellowship of like-minded people, living in a new society, enables one to prevail over the contradictions and turmoils of this present time, both as a newly centered individual and as a member of a supporting, affirming society. It is no wonder that many persons, some former alcoholics and dope addicts, have "switched" and have found some degree of serenity—some sense of personal worth—in religion as preached by evangelists. They may have lost all faith in themselves, and they may have felt, justifiably, the rejection of friends and family, but in the eyes of God, they are persons of infinite worth. Thus such preaching reaches out to genuine needs. Even the requirement that one accept one's guilt and subscribe to a strong moral code makes sense. Furthermore, the immediate fruits of ethical behavior, born of the certainty of conversion, are gratifying. One experiences a sense of joy, inner peace, serenity. Feelings of being lost, of having no center, of constant dissatisfaction with one's life, disappear. When preachers and converts testify to their new life-style, their sense of self-respect, and their growing capacity to handle life's problems, they become living proofs to those who hear them, that Jesus saves.

There is, finally, another element in this evangelistic theology of the sermon that touches a vital spot in a person's self-understanding and that is particularly applicable to America today—the emphasis upon individual decision and initiative. Indeed, it may be that evangelistic preaching offers a helpful critique to an understanding of our social nature, which tends today to be defined almost solely in strictly collective terms. For while preaching is conducted in a congregational setting, the message is really addressed to each individual. The implications are clear. Decision for Christ is a personal, private matter. It must and can be made in spite of social pressures on all sides that tend to shape a person into a "face in the crowd." Or it can be made in spite of the fact that one is born into a ghetto and is apparently doomed to repeat the past tragic story of poverty, drugs, and hopelessness. Each person is assured that he or she can, on his or her own initiative, break with the past and be born again. To be sure, one must confess one's own helplessness and admit that no human work merits Christ's atoning gift of himself. However, this understanding of oneself is already acknowledged privately by the one who suffers and it becomes a personal confession to Christ, whose demands in terms of a moral code are seen as promising a new life. In deciding for Christ, one acquires a new identity, becoming acceptable to oneself and to Christ. This act is something done and at the same time, something given. Faith, in this sense, is both a personal act and a decision made by God in Christ, from the beginning. A person then understands him- or herself as a being—a soul—apart from all the sociological descriptions applied by society. I suggest that such an attitude carries a strong appeal to persons seeking a vital center or a source or standard by which they may achieve some sense of personal worth.

V. BLACK LIBERATIONISM: ALBERT B. CLEAGE, JR.

We have come together to commemorate the triumphal entry of the Black Messiah into Jerusalem.

Albert B. Cleage, Jr.

I am not sure at this point that one can predict the future of black liberation theology. The movement is still gathering strength and advocates, and books and articles seek to shape its contours and give it flesh and substance.[1] I do know, however, that in the sermons of Albert Cleage, one can find an articulate black theology which, after more than a decade, deserves a fresh look. The sermons represent a conscious, reasoned decision to proclaim a black Messiah, in order to build up a new community of God's chosen people. Cleage's understanding of the sermon and its purpose is well worth our attention. In his own way, he is asking the same questions raised by the other theologies of preaching examined in this book and is offering his own answers. Those answers are not shared in their totality by most black theologians and preachers today, but they predate and still profoundly influence black preaching.

In his sermon "Dr. King and Black Power," Cleage announces his theme in this manner: "We have come together to commemorate the triumphal entry of the Black Messiah into Jerusalem two thousand years ago, and to pay tribute to Dr. Martin Luther King, a black leader."[2] On Thursday evening of the preceding week, King had been murdered by a white man in Memphis, Tennessee. The sermon deals with that horrifying event in the context of Palm Sunday, for Cleage sees an essential relationship between King's murder and Jesus' entry into Jerusalem. One is conscious at once of a determined effort to show a significant relationship between those two historic persons and the events that shaped their destinies and brought about their executions, and to relate the events of two thousand years past to contemporary America. This sermon is a conscious attempt to rethink exegesis and theology in terms of blacks, who are caught up in a power struggle with the white community. The sermon is an attempt to make the good news of the gospel relevant to an enslaved people—people who, in the idiom of many black preachers, have been enslaved by Pharaoh and ordered to live out a hopeless existence. How, precisely, does Cleage go about this task, and what does he feel eventuates from this kind of sermon?

THE CENTRALITY OF PREACHING

It should be noted from the outset that in the worship of the black church, the sermon is the focal point toward which all else leads, and from which all else follows. The agonies and ecstasies of the black sermon must be experienced. They are difficult to describe in prose, for they bear more resemblance to poetry or song. Preacher and congregation become caught up in a common bond of suffering and release as the scripture and the preacher's interpretation of it become, for all present, a living recital of their own despair and hope. All this is communicated through a blend of word and chant, invitation and response, in which both preacher and congregation are totally involved. The pitch of excitement rises as the preacher's voice scales another octave. Encouragements are offered by the congregation. The preacher asks for prayer, and members respond. All are locked in a struggle to heighten the growing awareness of the presence of the Spirit who exorcises demons and offers release from the agonies that afflict them all. The event is prepared for, awaited, expected. It is in some sense contrived, as are all happenings; still, the event is more than the sum of its parts. The preacher knows what he is doing, as does the congregation, and the process is necessary if there is to be a genuine experience. Certainly the sermon is the essential expression of black worship.

This is the situation in which Cleage and the people he serves function. It seems to me, however, that Cleage wishes to use the sermon for purposes other than those traditionally developed in black worship. What we find here is the beginning of a new tradition in preaching, whose roots are acknowledged, but whose futurism is rejected. Preaching is to be neither of the storefront variety or of the rising middle-class black-bourgeoise type.

In order to understand this anomaly it is important to point out that black preaching traditionally developed a unique sense of correspondence between the textual situation in which the sermon was rooted and the existing situation of the gathered community. Blacks understood themselves to be an enslaved people who found the strength to survive because of the freedom promised by God. The sermon reinforced this conviction; the community relived enslavement and freedom every Sunday. History was brought forward, and the past was reenacted as the people identified with persons and events in the biblical narratives. Personalities such as Moses, Pharaoh, Mary, and Jesus, as well as places such as Jordan and Heaven, were genuine persons and locations. Through the sermon event, the distance between the past and the present collapsed, and worship became an enactment in their present of the promises given by God in the past. The sufferings of Israel and those of the black community were fused, so that both, as it were, inhabited the same time and place.

However, as enslavement continued and hope of the freedom and justice promised in the Bible seemed less and less possible, "heaven" became more and more related to life after death. The overwhelming power of enslavement; the inability to establish any power-base in order to respond to injustice effectively; the sheer pressure of oppression dampened hopes for God's future as a historical reality. A theology of hope developed, which projected a future of justice into eternal life and at the same time provided an energy and a spirit that enabled life to go on.[3]

For Cleage, the task of the sermon is to retrieve the realm of salvation from life beyond the grave and to place it where it belongs, in the here and now. The "eternal now" of Tillich's sermons is to become the "historical now." To this end, the content of the sermon deals with daily events as blacks experience them in a white world. The justification for this approach is to be found in the biblical texts that are the bases for preaching. The promise of a future life of peace and joy beyond the grave is an interpretation of Christianity read through white eyes and designed to maintain a people in bondage as long as possible. To Cleage, white Christianity is, after all, little more than an ideological support for servitude. Blacks have been baptized—that is, mind-washed—into a religion that has little to do with what Jesus taught, what he did, or the people to whom he addressed his message.

There were a number of exegetical moves that made this shift in direction and intention possible. We shall discuss this process in some detail, but first let us trace its development in "Dr. King and Black Power."

> Our scripture text this morning is taken from the Gospel of Luke, the 19th chapter, the 39th and 40th verses. Jesus, the Black Messiah, was going to Jerusalem. He knew that he was going to be killed, that the Toms and white folks, the Gentiles, were going to get together and kill him.[4]

The reader will notice at once the significant use of language in this typical segment of the sermon. The Palm Sunday text is so stated and commented upon as to establish a blending, if not merging, of that traditional account with contemporary events.

The situation is revolutionary—a power struggle between blacks and the white establishment (the Gentile world). Jesus is considered to be the leader of this revolution and is determined to overthrow the establishment. Some, we hear, hail his entry as God's will. "Blessed be the King who comes in the name of the Lord." But the whites—the Pharisees—realize that he threatens their power-base and plot to destroy him. Their plan is to have him assassinated, just as the white establishment in America murdered Martin Luther King. In doing this, they consciously and willfully pervert the plan of the black Messiah, who believes and teaches that it is God's will that black people should be free—not in some future time, but now.

On first inspection, this attempt to relate events in the life and teachings of Jesus to the present age seems no different from the strategies employed by liberals. There is much more here, however, than meets the eye. When sermons from white liberal pulpits urge people to love their neighbors and deal justly with the poor and oppressed, the implication is that the listeners should go out and do something for the have-nots of this world. The congregation is to be moved by compassion for the poor and, in the tradition of the good Samaritan, heal the wounds of the world for Christ's sake. Whites are to offer to blacks the benefits of their faith and works for the sake of justice.

Nothing like this is being said in Cleage's sermons, even though there is the common concern for justice. The word "black," as descriptive of Jesus' self-understanding and deeds, is the key symbol. What is really being most skillfully communicated, is that the have-nots—the oppressed—are the very people with whom Jesus identifies. The oppressed are the chosen people, and the whites have nothing to offer them but trouble. Indeed, in this sense, Jesus is "black"; it is for his own people that he suffered and sought to establish a new nation. That nation is not being called to take the message and deeds of justice to others, but to hear the good news that Jesus is really their brother who has come to save them. He too knew suffering, rejection, alienation, and was martyred for his beliefs and actions. He came to set black people free and to enable them to achieve justice for themselves. It is the white community that is the enemy. Indeed, one might go on to say that white people cannot hear this message in the texts because they do not consider themselves oppressed. They are not persecuted, hounded, pressed into ghettoes, and condemned to lives of perpetual poverty.

Cleage's message, then, does not appeal to the conscience of a community, but rather to its sense of mission in terms of its own salvation. There is no attempt to evoke feelings of guilt or a sense of personal sin. Rather, the accent falls almost totally on the call for people to identify with the purpose of Jesus' entry into Jerusalem and to become members of that group. Jesus did not die upon a cross in order to take away the sins of the world. He died because he resisted the powers and principalities of an evil world—the white world. In doing so, he demonstrated that this path of confrontation and resistance, even to death, is the will of God and for the sake of the black nation. His death has meaning because it enables a new community to develop. Suffering is not a duty one takes upon oneself as an ethical obligation; it is not a good work. It is rather the path that leads to the creation of a new nation and that therefore confers meaning upon all life. The congregation is not called upon to put itself in the shoes of the poor and oppressed and thus, by a stretch of the imagination and the exertion of a guilty conscience, to identify with them or do something for them. No, the real community of God is made up of the rejected themselves. To be black is to follow the black Messiah; it is to see this identification in oneself and in others in the congregation.

This means then that the function of the sermon is to build up the community. It seeks to foster black identity by showing that Jesus was black, as were those Jews who, under the influence of Moses, left Egypt and established a new nation. "Black" in this sense is a term that at times obviously refers to skin color but also symbolizes people who have experienced suffering and alienation. It must be seen by the congregation as a symbol of dignity and worth. It connotes self-love and beauty.

> You can't build dignity in black people if they go down on their knees every day, worshiping a white Jesus and a white God. We are going to communicate with black churches. We are going to talk with them, reason with them, shame them if nothing else works, saying, "Accept the historic fact. Christianity is our religion."[5]

The blending of the Palm Sunday text, Jesus' entry into Jerusalem, with the death of Martin Luther King is an intentional exegetical decision. It is not made in isolation from a biblical view and occasioned by this one event alone, but is rather part of Cleage's whole theology. Jesus calls the people to confront the power establishment, as King did. Black leaders have learned, thanks to his prophetic leadership, that black people can unite, fight, and die for the things they believe in. That is, they can die for some creative purpose, but not as mere tools of the white establishment. Blacks, under King's leadership, were beginning to feel that they were becoming a people and that they could stand up against the white world. The difficult struggle ahead is "to get the brothers and the sisters together." To do this, they must overcome their feelings of helplessness and hopelessness engendered by centuries of defeat. The building of an effective community is a political and economic effort calling for sacrifice, even to the point of death. This goal and the actions necessary to achieve it are not only urgent and obvious present tasks lying before the people—they are at the same time consonant with the call of Jesus.

This new style of preaching, together with the program enunciated in almost every sermon, is a conscious departure from the black theology of former times that was associated with storefront religion. Cleage feels that religion develops a style and content in order to meet people's needs; it fashions a theology in tune with the times in which people live. Thus it can be said that the black church of another era did meet the genuine needs of an enslaved people. "All the shouting and the emotionalism that people laugh about offered an escape from oppression and we had to have some kind of escape. . . . From somewhere we had to find strength to get through another week."[6]

Now, however, the black community recognizes the weaknesses and deceptions in that kind of preaching. The catharsis experienced may have relieved the pain momentarily, but it did nothing to change the conditions that brought it about. It was truly an opiate of the people. Furthermore, it was this very religion that contributed to the agonies it claimed to assuage. For black religion was based upon a white Christianity which fostered feelings of personal guilt, urged people to love their neighbors, to turn the other cheek, to walk the second mile, and to accept the status quo. All this is to be cast out—thrown away as a series of lies. A theology of hope that is worth anything should foster a sense of self-respect and the promise of a new life-style *now*. It is the will of God that black people should be free. All the shouting and emotionalism should grow out of that personal conviction, because what is offered is truly a liberating theology.

Blackness, community, power: These three images are the conscious subject matter of the sermons, which are biblical in their roots, giving black people a sense of pride in themselves based upon the assurance that they are a chosen people and offering theological justification for overthrow of the establishment. Cleage's preaching is an abrupt departure from traditional black preaching and a rejection of stereotyped white Christianity, with its misuse of the Bible.

This shift may be illustrated very well by the way Cleage deals with the issue of violence, particularly in the sermon concerning Martin Luther King and black power. Cleage argues that King's policy of nonviolence resulted in his own death by violent means. Nonviolence therefore does not work; it begets violence and offers no constructive road to freedom. Actually, as Cleage interprets King's role, what King did achieve, whether intended or not, was the development of a strong community of blacks. And in the process of challenging the establishment and organizing a power-base, he accomplished another vital goal. While King talked about redemptive suffering and believed in it himself, "what he said had no relationship to what was happening in the hearts and minds and souls of black people."[7] It was really not the goal of redemptive suffering that he engendered in their hearts, but black courage. King's real legacy to the future is the establishment of a sense of worth and a courage to achieve goals of justice.

The basic difference between Cleage and King may be stated in terms of the concepts of love and justice. King's theology developed out of a concern that Christian love shape and dominate political and social action, while for Cleage, the priority is upon justice, as seen in the deeds and words of Jesus.

> We can't go to the white man and ask him to love us. We've done it too long. It's futile. We want justice, and we are going to fight for justice. We don't even think about love. Love is only something for inside the Nation. . . . Outside the Nation we are not thinking about love. We are thinking only about justice.[8]

Actually, this determination to set forth a vital relationship between the aims and actions of Jesus and the present struggle for black liberation is imperative, from the point of view of many black church leaders today. Defection from churches by young blacks, both in the ghetto and on the college campus, is alarming. For all too many of these young men and women, the "white" Jesus has little to say. Indeed, "whiteness" is a basic hindrance to hearing the gospel at all; it is a constant visual reminder of servitude; it both attracts and repels blacks. For generations they have been conned into seeking identity by becoming "white"; by taking on white virtues and believing white myths about their economic and social future, as well as about religious teachings, they thought they would be able to enter the mainstream of white society. That was the hope and assurance of Booker T. Washington. The naiveté of this posture is overwhelming as one reviews the nation's history. Blacks believed they could trust white people because the whites were Christians. That trust turned into nightmares for many blacks, and their response is aptly called black rage.[9]

It is in this connection that the question of Jesus' identity becomes crucial. By referring to Jesus as the black Messiah, Cleage hopes that a black person's quest for identity can be realized in a black church led by the black Jesus. There is still a great possibility for a religious renewal in the black church, Cleage affirms, but it must be harnessed and developed by a theology that meets the needs of the age. The sermon is to be an essential means of accomplishing that objective.

THE CHOSEN PEOPLE

It might be said that Cleage's understanding of the sermon's message and of the theology that shapes it is drawn solely from the daily struggles of black people. Indeed, the sermon quoted at some length in this chapter spends most of its energy and content on a discussion of Martin Luther King and Malcolm X and the way in which Jesus' teachings relate to those two men. However, it is all too easy to level charges of eisegesis and to dismiss the sermons as unbiblical. The charge that people simply see in the Bible what they want to see and that they use the texts to justify their own points of view, may be leveled at us all. Actually, Cleage's sermons do reveal a developed theology—an attempt to put together a total picture of the Bible's message.

> But our religion is something different. The black man's religion is essentially based on the Old Testament concepts of the nation of Israel, God's chosen people, and our knowledge that the problems of the black Israelites were the same as ours. When we read the Old Testament, we can identify with a black people who were guided and loved by God. Everything in the Old Testament speaks to our problem.[10]

This is a typical statement by Cleage; let us look at it carefully. It is clear that Cleage means that, just as the "black Israelites" were chosen by God, so are black people today. Moses was "black." "The Bible was written by black Jews. The Old Testament is the history of black Jews" who wandered in the wilderness for forty years and fought their way into the promised land. Here we come upon a basic theme to which Cleage returns time and again and which carries many meanings—the notion of being chosen.

To be chosen confers dignity upon a people—not upon individuals, but in a collective or corporate sense. Individuals receive their identity from the group. They receive their sense of worth from participating in and sharing the aims of the group—that is, the church. "As a black people, we don't have a lot of separate dignities. We have one dignity. . . . We have got to find dignity somewhere because we will never be a nation until we can first build some sense of dignity."[11]

To be chosen not only confers dignity but also shapes the purpose and destiny of the "nation." It is the black nation that is called by God to realize a new world order. It is black people—the alienated, rejected, and oppressed—who are called to establish justice on earth. It is with them that God has made an everlasting covenant. To have this knowledge; to identify with the promises of God is to receive a new strength for the task ahead. "We could look the white man straight in the eye and say, 'There is nothing you can do to destroy us.' "[12]

To be chosen also means to be obligated to act out in daily life the examples of ethical living found in the Old Testament. For Cleage, Moses' struggle with the Egyptians provides a model for contemporary action. Just as Moses struggled in a tense political situation to free his people, even to the extent of committing a senseless act of violence, so must blacks today struggle for freedom against a Pharaoh who forces them to make bricks without straw.

To be chosen means to give up one's false identity and to incorporate oneself into the community. To young people, Cleage presents the challenge, How shall I use my life? This is his contemporary interpretation of the call that came to the prophet Isaiah. Will I deny my blackness—deny my responsibility to the black nation—and strive for the pleasures and comforts of the white world? There are all too many young blacks who are "honkie-oriented"; they like "big cars and fine clothes." In other words, they are being sucked into the white establishment; they become "Toms." These tactics are used by whites to destroy blacks. The black person who would find his or her life must first lose it; the black life that has been shaped by the white world must be destroyed, for it is destroying that person.

To be chosen means to be separate, apart—unmixed with Canaan. Here Cleage defends and justifies his belief that separatism, not integration, is the goal of the black church. That goal, he believes, is in keeping with the will of God as proclaimed in both the Old and the New Testaments. Just as there are separate religions for white people and for black people, so there are entirely separate ways of life that distinguish them. God was angered by Israel's tendency to dilute its racial purity by mixing with heathen nations. In Canaan, the land the Israelites conquered, the Jews mixed with the people; and in Babylon, the land of captivity, the Jews again mixed with their captors—so much so that when the time for deliverance was at hand, the Jews were reluctant to leave. "And then the prophet stood up and said, 'You've got to separate from the people of the land. We must keep the Jews pure.' "[13] Cleage argues that the Jewish people, because of this history of intermarriage, are themselves a divided and confused nation; there are white Jews and black Jews today. The use of "black" and "white" here seems not to be a reference to skin color but is an indication of a sense of separate identity. At any rate, the message is clear enough to those who share Cleage's views. Now in our time, the temptation once again is to become "white"—that is, heathen. This, in Cleage's view, is the root sin of Israel. Integration subverts values and submerges identity. It atomizes the community and weakens the impulse to share its aims. It is the curse of individuals who go their own way and remain at ease in captivity. The prophets spoke, saying, "You have departed from the teachings of God. You are corrupt. You have lost your unity. You are no longer concerned about each other. Each person is living for himself alone."[14]

The tendency to mix with foreign peoples proved to be the downfall of Israel. In Cleage's view, the nation had degenerated into a group of individuals and had lost its identity. Some had gone over to the Romans—that is, to decode his language, had become "white." It was into this situation that the message and purpose of Jesus, set forth in the New Testament, were proclaimed. The picture of Jesus that Cleage sees in the Gospels emerges frequently throughout his sermons and forms a consistent pattern.

Jesus was the leader of a revolutionary movement, who went from village to village, preaching, teaching, healing, performing miracles—anything to get a group of people together so that he might give them his simple message. "It is necessary that you turn your back on individualism and join with your brothers to again build a black nation of which you can be proud."[15] Cleage believes that Jesus' disciples were Zealots, active in a revolutionary movement, and that John the Baptist was also a part of the movement. In fact, Cleage surmises that Jesus was influenced by John, shared his goals and activities, and at John's death, took over the leadership of the movement.

During his ministry Jesus struggled with the scribes and Pharisees who collaborated with Rome, and eventually this activity precipitated his death on the cross. Jesus also encountered resistance from his own people, because they were passive and did not want to become involved. They did not want to anger the establishment and at the same time, they felt their powerlessness as a personal disgrace, evoking in them a sense of shame and helplessness. "How can anyone rebuild a nation out of this? Out of our degradation, our corruption, our fear, our inadequacy. Oh, we have a few people who are doing well, but for the most part, we are poverty-stricken, we are helpless. How can anyone build a Nation out of this?"[16] Even Jesus' family and close friends and associates turned against him, thinking he must be mad to threaten the established order. At the same time, those people knew in their hearts that they too ought to be willing to stand up and fight. Hence the characteristic ambivalence of black people—a chosen but oppressed people who themselves have become the greatest obstacle to the building of their own nation.

Nevertheless, in spite of opposition from all sides, Jesus went about setting up a revolutionary movement, for which he selected twelve disciples; that was the beginning of the nation. Now Cleage outlines what he believes to be the strategy of the movement and describes the circumstances that led to Jesus' passion and death. While there are many references to elements of this narration scattered throughout the sermons, Cleage's most consistent development is found in another Palm Sunday sermon, "He Stirs Up the People."

Jesus had been preaching for some time when he decided to go to Jerusalem to confront the powers and authorities. His activities had, of course, aroused opposition. He and his followers were constantly on the move; even remaining in small villages overnight was perilous, and he often was forced to find rest in the countryside, where he hid and prayed. Jesus knew he would be assassinated, but he was determined to make his final act of commitment a public affair. Too many black leaders, according to Cleage, have been killed in secret, thus preventing them from becoming martyrs. But "Jesus realized that it was not fitting that a prophet should die outside of Jerusalem. . . . So he decided to go right into the middle of Jerusalem and do what he had to do, and if they were going to kill him, they would have to do it there where everybody could see and understand."[17] His entry into Jerusalem was hailed as a "nationalistic demonstration" by those who understood it. His cleansing of the temple was a clear expression of his righteous anger against the money changers, and it was this public act that decided Jesus' fate, though the scribes and Pharisees were not at that moment sure of their strength and feared the crowds who hailed him.

Later on, these same religious leaders engaged in a debate with Jesus, attempting to prove that he was disloyal. It was not his religious teachings that basically concerned them, but rather the political threat he represented in his movement to build a nation. However, their attempt failed, and Jesus continued to preach, hoping to keep up the momentum of nation-building. He shared one final meal with his disciples, during which he tried "to get them to understand that the Nation can come into being only when we are willing to sacrifice and be humble."[18] His symbolic footwashing and the breaking of bread were accompanied by specific teachings as to how the twelve were to behave after his death. The Communion service words of institution called for a total dedication to the nation. "This is my body broken for you. You must also be willing to have your body broken for the Nation." In this manner, Jesus predicted his crucifixion. Thus "Jesus was crucified because he tried to bring a Black Nation into being."[19] It is not possible to understand the subsequent resurrection apart from this interpretation of Jesus' death, according to Cleage, for the resurrection is the resurrection of a nation.

This is the true message of Jesus—the meaning of his life, death and resurrection—and it must be recovered, Cleage says. It has been concealed for two thousand years, due mainly to the work of the apostle Paul, a Jew who organized the church and sought to convert other peoples. In doing so, he changed the message in order to make it acceptable to the Gentiles—the white people—who were under the influence of heathen religions. To realize how this paganism altered the real meaning of Jesus' life and work, we should compare the Gospel of Mark with that of John. The Gospel of John took on the pagan philosophy of the Gentiles and tried to fit it into the life of Jesus. The historic Jesus was completely lost. Paul furthermore transformed the Christian faith into an individualistic, private affair, concerned with sin, guilt, and the need for personal salvation. This religion is in no way related to the mission of Jesus, for it directs the believer's concern solely to a life after death. It was this understanding of Jesus that was taken over by western (white) Christianity and handed on to the slaves. It is then the task of black people today to recover what Jesus really said and did, for white Christianity "is not the religion of Jesus. This is not the religion of Israel. In it, the concept of the Nation is destroyed. . . . Even though we have been confused by this corruption, when we go back to the Bible, we must search for the religion of Jesus, the Black Messiah."[20]

AN APPRAISAL

An interpretation of Jesus as a revolutionary prophet is not new in the history of biblical studies, nor is the decision to single out the apostle Paul as the chief defector from the real message of Jesus' life. What is new is the carefully delineated and conscious attempt to identify the experience of black people today with that of the Jews in both Old and New Testaments. The interweaving of past events and persons with the contemporary experience of a suffering people is remarkably consistent and arresting. The account developed by Cleage initially strikes whites as strange, foreign—alien to their own experience. This, if Cleage is right, is because they do not know what it is to be oppressed or are so caught up in a privatized faith that they are incapable of seeing or experiencing Christianity's revolutionary dimension. This would be the most tolerant interpretation. Another is that the revolutionary aspects of Jesus' message are indeed all too clear and must somehow be reinterpreted in order to maintain the present power distribution in society.

Cleage's understanding of the sermon itself is fascinating, for he sees it as the means by which the church or nation is to be built up. It is not an isolated event in the service of public worship, directed to individuals, but rather an integral part of a grand design. The sermon is a call for people to find identity with Jesus and one another, and to participate in the struggle against "the man." It calls for "conversion"—getting rid of white attitudes; this is not some inner transformation in the soul, but the eradication of white thinking and life-style.

Furthermore, by using contemporary language peculiar to the black struggle for justice and relating it to the biblical language, he has enabled people to identify with texts and to experience them as descriptions of their own situation. One has only to read the poem-sermons of James Weldon Johnson in *God's Trombones*, to see this essential connection with the past; the distance between the past and present is collapsed. One can hardly read these sermons without being struck forcibly by their relevance, their timeliness, their attempt to face up to the problems and struggles of a people who are suffering and who need salvation now.[21]

It is perhaps just this felt need to make the gospel relevant that raises problems. In seeking to find the true Jesus in the Gospels, for the sake of preaching to this time, has Cleage in effect adopted a strategy he himself deplores? It is his own charge that Paul, in order to present a religion to a people not familiar with the Jewish faith, changed its meaning in order to acquire conversions. May one not fairly level the same charge against Cleage? Does he have his own canon within the canon? Has he selected one dimension of the Gospel accounts and accepted it as the criterion by which to measure the authenticity of all else in the texts? Has this been done solely because of the present situation in which blacks find themselves? Are the biblical accounts to be evaluated and justified only to the extent that they bear witness to, explain, and support the agonies and frustrations of black people in America?

That this well may be the case is particularly evident in Cleage's treatment of the themes of love and justice, confrontation and reconciliation. Certainly his understanding, based upon the teaching of Jesus, is a judgment upon the notions of justice practiced by white Christianity—not only toward blacks, but toward Native Americans and Chicanos as well. It may be asked though, whether Cleage has not screened out much in Jesus' teachings and deeds that deals with reconciliation? If so, these texts stand as a judgment upon Cleage. It is one thing to argue that white Christians use Christian love and reconciliation as devices to pacify blacks. It is another to deny that God wills love and that he desires the unification of all people. One might say, in general terms, that Cleage's sermons preach judgment and lack grace.

One detects real ambivalence in Cleage's theories pertaining to the matter of violence. To what extent is a Christian justified in taking up arms, participating in riots and looting, and resisting the police? One notes the same problem in emerging forms of liberation theology in Latin America, South Africa, and Zimbabwe. In short, one is dealing with a question of ends and means. This matter is developed in detail in James H. Cone's book *Black Theology and Black Power*, and is not properly material for this discussion, except to observe that a belief in ethics, in addition to beliefs about God and Jesus, is crucial in relation to the sermon. [22]

What is a viable theology for black Christians today? What theology would speak to the agonies of life in a perpetual ghetto? Answers given by white Christians all too often proceed from dogmatic positions already worked out in terms of their own experience. But are not these much too culture-bound assumptions? For many such people, well intentioned though they may be, the question is, How does one apply the Christian faith to a new situation? For blacks, the question is quite different: What is the gospel of Jesus Christ?

Cleage's sermons call preachers to begin all over again—in this time, under these conditions—to recover what has been lost. The Bible can no longer be perceived as a western, white interpretation, conceiving of Jesus of Nazareth as a white man.

VI. DEVELOPING A THEOLOGY TO PREACH

By now it should be clear that preaching the gospel of Jesus Christ involves serious theological reflection on our part. As we have seen in previous chapters, there is wide divergence among preachers as to the content of that gospel and as to the general purpose of preaching itself. We all preach the crucified Christ, but the meaning of that proclamation is the subject of considerable difference of interpretation. Let us consider the way the person of Jesus Christ is treated in the theologies we have discussed and the effect this has had upon the substance, intention, and even the tone of the sermons. As we do this, let us also examine our preferences, for clues to our own beliefs. Isolating and examining our beliefs enables us to begin the process of consciously developing our own "preaching theology." This is, of course, an ongoing task begun in a formal way in seminary but, I hope, continued throughout our professional careers.

JESUS CHRIST—THE ONLY MESSAGE

Barth's theology, perhaps more than any of the others we have discussed, seeks to root our thinking and our lives in the announcement that Jesus is God among us. He is God's self-revelation—not an example of a dedicated person deeply moved and persuaded by God, but God's own person in human form. The only significant subject for preaching, therefore, is Jesus Christ. For this reason, Barth sets aside the question of relevance—that is, concern for the human situation and for the needs people express. This is not because he fails to recognize them as part of the context in which sermons occur, but because he believes that the prior concern is God's movement toward us, not our movement toward God. The Bible is not the story of our quest for God, but of God's quest for us. We may wish to proclaim the humanity of Jesus—to show how much Jesus resembles us—and that would not be wrong. Barth, on the other hand, stresses not the humanity of Jesus, but the humanity of God in the person of Jesus. He became like us, that we might become like him. What is called for in preaching then, is a radical reassessment of ourselves, culminating in our confession that without God's self-revelation, we can never in any sense know who God in Jesus Christ is for us. Barth's sermons deal movingly and compassionately with our human situation, but they assert that we are helpless to save ourselves, although we are endlessly tempted to think that we can. Nevertheless, this gloomy evaluation of human potential does not result in grim forecasts about a destructive future. Indeed, the predominant mood of the sermons is one of rejoicing. This is so because Barth's theology centers in the wonder of the Incarnation—the coming of Jesus Christ! I can think of no better way to feel this quality than to listen to the Sinfonia in Cantata II of Bach's *Christmas Oratorio*. It expresses in wondrous tones the descending movement and the presentiment of dawn, followed shortly by the magnificent chorale, "Break forth, oh beauteous light of dawn,/and let the heavens become light!" All this to simple shepherds!

Who is Jesus to the evangelists? We do not read in their sermons of the wonder of Christmas, but of the wonder of the cross. Above all else in their sermons, Jesus is the Man who died on the cross for our sins. In his blood, we are saved. He atoned for us all, and it is this miraculous self-sacrifice that enables us now to be cleansed of our sins, if we will but believe. The God revealed to us in this scenario of the sacred story pays the price, and though destroyed, he overcomes Satan through the resurrection. It is in the events of Good Friday and Easter—particularly of Good Friday—that the central theology of preaching is shaped in this tradition. And this tradition tends to shape the form of the sermons; it sets the mood and tonal quality. Converts attest that Jesus died for them, and the knowledge and acceptance of that sacrifice has made all the difference in the world to them. Jesus paid the price for their sins. In some sense, he was their substitute, taking their place and dying for them, once and for all.

Beyond this, Jesus is often viewed as the supreme Law Giver, setting up standards for behavior. His teachings offer guides for our conduct in daily life; they tell us how to behave and set before us a way of living that can culminate in eternal life. The tone of such preaching, then, is a combination of urgency and moral earnestness. Something dramatic may happen—can happen! This hour of preaching is fraught with sacred possibilities.

To liberals, the humanity of Jesus the Son of God who also is the Son of man, is most important. Jesus, in his words and deeds, points the way to and is, in some sense, a manifestation of the kingdom of God. Jesus is the great Prophet, whose total being was given over to the will of God for the sake of the world. His words and deeds constitute examples of the totally dedicated life, lived out for the poor, the oppressed, the sick, and the helpless. Jesus' death on the cross is the supreme example of one life given up for others. His death shows us how much he loves us and cares for us. His life shows us how we should live, for the sake of the kingdom of God.

"Christ himself is Christianity," says Fosdick. He means that in the person of Jesus we see the magnificent possibilities of human existence made flesh in the world. The accent on the humanity of Jesus is purposefully stressed in order to rescue him from titles and doctrinal formulations which tend to make him a complicated figure in a theological system. Indeed, one might say, when comparing this emphasis with Barth's theology, that the liberals begin with Jesus in order to make contact with God, whereas Barth attempts something like the reverse—we cannot know who Jesus is until we confess that he is God and dwelt among us.

The Jesus who appears in liberal preaching is not so much the Man on the cross as the Man in the marketplace, whose life for others awakens in us an enthusiasm for changing the world by following in his steps. We meet Jesus in such sermons "where the action is," and rejoice together when injustice is defeated. Far from emphasizing the difference between Jesus and ourselves, they tend to stress the human potential for becoming Christ-like. They appeal to conscience and instill confidence in the possibility of making neighbors out of our enemies and of eliminating the social evils that society and individuals have created.

For blacks during the period of slavery, Jesus was the one person with whom they could identify. "Nobody knows the troubles I've seen; nobody knows but Jesus." However, the Jesus whom Cleage proclaims as the black Messiah, whose life and deeds he sees in the New Testament, is a different person. Blacks had identified with Jesus because he, too, suffered unbelievably in the hands of an oppressive society. He knew of their agonies, and in his presence they found One who dealt with them as human beings, not as slaves. He knew too of their helplessness, and his promises offered them a real future—if not in this life, certainly in the life to come. But the Jesus Cleage preaches is a revolutionary leader who calls upon blacks, as his chosen people, to throw off the bonds of oppression now and to create a new life for themselves. The new song is, "We will overcome—now!" The mood of this theme is one of active participation in a struggle for justice, as compared to the passive, painful, resigned mood of another generation of black preaching, which found joy in heaven and hell on earth. The Jesus that Cleage sees in the Bible has been carefully hidden by the white world, and one can trace this distortion in the texts themselves. Cleage is not alone in this approach, for there are others who argue that in Jesus, one sees the justification for political revolution.[1]

Thus blacks, in Cleage's sermons, are urged to identify with Jesus, not so much in his suffering, as in his struggle for justice. He is more than the Man who suffered on the cross; he is the Leader in the streets, who calls his people to follow him. In following Jesus, one obtains one's real identity, for he is the black Messiah who has come to lead his chosen people, blacks. The tone of these sermons is strident, angry, provocative. They are calculated to energize people; to awaken them to their real sense of identity and purpose in life. Their enthusiasm should be directed to the battle for justice. Sermons are preached for the sake of building up the church, which, in its mission and structures, is to be the place where strategies and tactics for battle are planned.

One may feel called to reject this view of Jesus as being one-sided, but the struggle in Latin America and the emergent expressions of liberation theology there should give us pause. Certainly the homilies of Pope John Paul II, preached during his trip to Latin America, were listened to with the greatest attention. He attempted on the one hand to give encouragement to oppressed people and to justify their hunger for justice. At the same time, he sought to find some middle ground when it came to the question of the means to that end. Jesus' teaching is certainly revolutionary, but his apparent rejection of violence, as superbly witnessed to by the cross, suggests that the New Testament does not condone violence as a way to achieve freedom and justice. At least this much is clear: Sermons addressed to historical conditions concerning a people's life are listened to. The apparent dilemma is that the person of Jesus and the words and deeds that characterized his ministry do not lend themselves easily to blueprints for political and social action. One may quote passages of scripture that apparently justify violent action, and others that do not.

The Jesus we preach about is very likely to be an interpretation shaped, whether or not we are conscious of it, by our own situation, the historical context, and the felt needs of the time. I was once assisting a student in his effort to read texts more creatively. The text used for practice was a passage from Matthew's Gospel, in which Jesus severely castigates the Pharisees, heaping abuse upon them in no uncertain terms. The student found it almost impossible to read that passage in the tone its content demanded. The reason was, it turned out, that he thought of Jesus as his "guru," mild and responsive, open and understanding. The almost abusive feeling-tone of the text simply affronted him and probably deeply disturbed an inner image of Jesus with which he had been living, perhaps unconsciously, for some time.

Who is Jesus in the sermons of Paul Tillich? Formally stated, he is "the Christ." Tillich almost always inserts the definite article between the two names. In doing so, I believe he wishes to make clear that Jesus is characterized by his openness to the power of being—to God, in the fullest possible sense. Jesus is the supreme symbol in Tillich's use of the word "God." He is translucent to God; the power of God shines through him fully. Perhaps one could say that this is Tillich's attempt to rethink the traditional creedal language, which affirms that Jesus is both Man and God, but that he must be thought of as God and in no sense as a subordinate being. At the same time, one has the feeling that in Tillich's sermons and other writings, Jesus becomes more a means of reaching God than being God. Like the symbol, Jesus' function is to point beyond himself to God. There is also a charismatic quality about the person of Jesus in Tillich's preaching. Power emanates from him and people are grasped by this energy. Perhaps one way of expressing this would be to suggest that the Jesus Tillich presents may be seen most clearly on the walls of catacombs. He is preeminently the Healer in catacomb art, and often in the sermons as well. The tone of the sermons is therapeutic; our felt relation to Jesus is more analogous to Counselor than to either Prophet or Judge. That, it seems to me, is because Tillich's approach to congregations is that of reflective consideration of our common concern, a shared quest for meaning. Jesus does not so much impart faith as he energizes or clarifies it in us. We who struggle for life's meaning are not unaware of the answer, but experience it in torn and often diabolic forms. Our sickness is known to us. And even when we deny that we need a healer, we can be helped to see that we do, if only the sermon can find the right language—the revealing metaphors, the analogies taken from our life—which can open up to us the healing potentialities present in Jesus. The tone of these sermons, therefore, is meditative, contemplative, directing us to quest inward; to examine our lives more earnestly. The process of finding Jesus the Christ begins, in this strategy of preaching, with finding ourselves—exposing ourselves to ourselves without fear. The sermons lay great emphasis upon the fact that our own understanding of life is a clue to our real nature. They appeal not so much to conscience or will or reason, but to our deeper feelings about ourselves. They press us downward into the depth of our self-perception; they probe for the self in its totality, as a fundamental picture of our real nature.

THE CHRISTOLOGICAL FOCUS

There is undoubtedly a hunger to hear the gospel preached clearly, simply, and understandably. There is, as well, the ever latent and often manifested complaint by congregations that sermons are too theological and do not present us with a clear picture of Jesus. Rex Humbard, the television evangelist, thrives on sermons that have a simple direct message, shorn of all theological niceties. He knows what people need, and he gives it to them. Yet, as this book has attempted to point out, there is no one simple picture of Jesus—no eternal set of truths transmitted through the ages, undiluted and uninterpreted. Indeed, a case may be made that the Bible itself reveals the struggle to proclaim and preach Jesus Christ, as filtered through the language, experience, and cultural situations to which it is addressed. "The Gospel," writes Ernst Käsemann, "simply isn't some timeless presence, but one which is always being reconstructed by compounding the past and by translation into the present, which is there to be won or lost."[2] The series of events that centered around the life, death, and resurrection of Jesus Christ, and the way those events constituted a new community, are attested to and proclaimed in the New Testament. They might be called the canon within the canon. They are the hard core of commitment to which all religious writers attest and confess. Their proclamation and explication themselves, however, are interpretations of those events. Indeed, one may even observe this process of interpretation at work in the biblical texts.

The texts that constitute the New Testament are confessions used in the early church to preach faith in Jesus Christ, to carry out missionary activity, to build up newly formed communities, to respond to critics and opponents, and finally, to encourage people who were undergoing persecution for their faith. In order to communicate this faith in a predominantly Jewish milieu, of which they themselves were a part, an essential relationship between Jesus Christ and the Old Testament was set forth through the process of proof texts. That is, the Old Testament was exegeted and interpreted from a theological point of view, as writers sought to show how, according to the Scriptures, Jesus Christ was the fulfillment of Old Testament prophecies. Indeed, the argument advanced by the evangelists, discussed in an earlier chapter, is precisely the reverse of what actually took place. It was not the predictive character of the Old Testament prophets that proved the truthfulness of New Testament claims. Unquestionably, the Gospel writers saw an inner and necessary connection, for the same God who called Moses is revealed fully in Jesus the Messiah. However, the movement of the argument to trace and affirm the connection is from the present to the past, not the reverse! One of the traditional Old Testament texts used during Advent is that of Isaiah 9:2: "The people who walked in darkness have seen a great light." That the prophet envisioned the dawn of a new day with the coming of the Messiah reflected his faith in the future in terms of the promises of God. It was the New Testament writers who saw in the person of Jesus the fulfillment of that expectation in a way that the prophet could not foresee. This is hardly to argue that Isaiah was wrong in his vision of the future. Rather it is simply that he himself was in the hands of God, whose purposes and intentions could not be contained in Isaiah's thoughts, language, world-view, and historical situation. Isaiah's prophecies contained more than he himself foresaw!

At the same time, it must be noted that the language of these declarations about Jesus was shaped by the historical situations in which they were written. Jesus is said to be typified in Old Testament figures who pointed prophetically to his coming. He was in the line of Moses, but a greater than Moses has come. He is the Messiah, and yet the traditional understandings of the role of the Messiah do not completely explain his deeds, the form of his death, or his resurrection. He is identified as the Son of man, and yet the exact nature of this identification is not precisely clear. He is associated with the approaching kingdom of God, and yet the interpretation of that kingdom's form, its time of appearance, and Jesus' relation to it are not without ambiguities. In short, the linguistic mediums available in Jewish thought, all used to communicate the gospel, become pointers that do not fully explain Jesus' presence or the ultimate meaning of what he accomplished. There is always the "more than" about him. The language available in the culture of the time did not obscure revelation; rather it disclosed the final mystery that no language can ultimately contain or reveal. This is the unfathomable mystery of the Christian faith, that "a completely human work is in the service of a completely divine work, and that both works exist together unseparate and yet different."[3]

When the gospel was proclaimed and preached in a predominantly non-Jewish community, the language employed no longer contained Jewish thought-forms. In order to preach to a community unfamiliar with themes of prophecy and fulfillment, or of the hope for the Messiah, writers turned to the language and thought-forms available in the Greek culture. This was necessary so that people might hear the gospel and understand what was being offered, in order to be able to decide for or against it. Now we read of Jesus the Christ and we discover the appropriation of a mythological framework current in Greek thought—a descending and ascending God—as a linguistic medium for preaching. In the New Testament proclamations about Jesus, then, we witness a series of traditions at work to communicate the gospel to different cultures. This shifting suggests that faith formulations themselves are translations and interpretations.

Accepting this understanding of the method of communicating the biblical message concerning Jesus Christ in the texts, we can see that the story of God's life with us in Christ is subject to a variety of interpretations and that these appear in the texts themselves. They also may be seen at work in the theologies of preaching discussed in this book. While we are called to preach in such a way that the good news about Jesus Christ may be heard in our congregations, we must at the same time recognize that this is a human work and that what we have to proclaim will be in some sense a distortion of or a limitation upon the fullness of the identity of Christ. The danger is ever present that we will adopt some one dimension of that story and shape everything else around it.

Consider, for example, the tendency in liberal preaching and in the sermons of Cleage to see Jesus primarily in prophetic—even revolutionary—terms. Unquestionably Jesus was a prophet and his words and deeds were revolutionary. The texts of the New Testament, however, go far beyond that image of his nature and work. Or think of Tillich's attempt to interpret the human situation in existentialistic terms and to find in that analysis of the human condition a bridge between ourselves and the writers of the Gospels. Is not such an understanding of the human condition shaped more by western thought and historical conditions than by the texts themselves? Is not existential thought too privatized? Does it do full justice to the conceptions of human nature proclaimed in the texts? Or, given the understanding of the role of language, can it be argued that the only proper medium for preaching is the repetition of biblical phrases, as is often the case in evangelistic sermons? Are we not called to reinterpret such words in order that the gospel may be understood? Isn't that the very concern of many people—namely, that religious language constitutes as much a hindrance as a help to hearing the message of a sermon? Certainly for blacks, many commonly used religious phrases and figures of speech constitute severe obstacles to hearing the gospel. Think of the translation of "doulos" as "slave," for instance. That well may be the exact translation of the word, but the connotation for blacks is that of the slave era, and it is next to impossible to filter out those historical experiences from an interpretation of the word itself. For many people there has occurred what T. S. Eliot once called a "disassociation of sensibilities." World-views of another era, which enabled one to picture God's movement toward us in terms of ascending and descending—a movement most beautifully expressed in the Apostle's Creed—are simply unimaginable today, try as people may to accommodate themselves to them. We may be forced to acknowledge that religious language is more poetic than prosaic in nature—that is, it is ambiguous in the sense that it gives rise to thought and reflection on many levels. It may be that to accept this possibility does not mean the loss of faith, but rather the opportunity to be grasped and opened to the gospel in a new way. Certainly all these concerns about what is to be preached and how one may preach are alive and current in seminaries and churches today. How can we best prepare ourselves to preach, then, in this particular age?

LEARNING TO PREACH: A THEOLOGICAL TASK

We are indeed fortunate to have before us as part of our heritage, rich traditions of preaching. They express the faithful and thoughtful attempts by preachers to awaken, energize, support, and challenge congregations to hear the good news again in their own time and place. Indeed, the unique characteristic of sermons is their subject matter: Jesus Christ, as proclaimed in the Bible. The unifying feature of all the theologies of preaching discussed in this book is their common allegiance to that task and opportunity. It is both a burden and a possibility.

Students too often feel overwhelmed by these traditions. One often hears the lament that the great age of preaching is past; that we are lesser lights, feeble reflections of a waning moon. Actually that need not be and is not the case at all. There is a good deal of creative preaching going on in churches today, presented by faithful, thoughtful, creative men and women who, in the words of Fosdick, quoted earlier, are attempting "to think the great faiths of the Gospel through in contemporary terms, and to harness the great dynamics of the Gospel to contemporary tasks." How then do we, starting out in this profession, conceive of this task? How do we prepare ourselves to preach effectively?

A theology of preaching that contains some wholeness, some integrity, and some consistency, begins with our own reflections upon our fundamental beliefs about the Christian story. What others have said and written can be of enormous help to us, but unless we ourselves have grappled earnestly with the content and scope of our own faith, we shall have no way of using creatively what others have said. Therefore, it seems to me that we need to view the study of preaching primarily as a theological concern, and not solely as a process of learning how to preach. The painful and glorious opportunity present in seminary education is that of developing one's own theological identity. But that process of growth in faith will not take place if we do not thoughtfully examine what we believe now as we enter this area of life. I mean that we must view ourselves and our beliefs as being significant. So often, it is the tendency of students to belittle their own experience and their own reflection, or to feel overburdened by the sheer weight of the past, or awed by the supposed authority of the teacher, or discouraged by a sense of their own inadequacy. Or they fall captive to gaudy language which, when repeated often enough, takes on the weight of truth. Or they put on the whole "armor of God" and can hardly move.

Actually, there can be no serious growth in theological awareness until our self-awareness is recognized and understood. When we know, in some objective, consciously developed sense, what we believe, then we are able to enter into a genuine conversation with the beliefs and reflections of others who compose the traditions of the faith we share. Rightly, the emphasis in theological education today is upon the role of the laity in the total life of the church. Much time and thought is given to the development of a genuine sharing of faith. Nevertheless, unless we know where we stand, we shall be tossed about to and fro, lifted up by the latest fad in thinking and depressed when its sensational immediacy no longer seems to support us.

This vital and essential self-awareness in faith needs to be balanced by the reminder that preachers tend to develop one or two doctrines and preach about them week in and week out. Even Luther had his favorite hobbyhorse—faith and works. He succeeded in finding this vital issue of his age everywhere in the Old and New Testaments, and even after an amazing and exciting commentary on a text, would launch into his primary concern. We found this to be true in our study of theologies of preaching in this book. Preachers who subscribe to "topical" preaching tend to fall into this trap. They rightly argue that one should preach with a view toward current concerns which perplex people and for which there is the hunger and the need for a religious response. All too often, however, preachers are highly selective, choosing only issues that interest them or bending texts to fit the topics selected. The danger involved in forcing texts to fit needs or in choosing texts that seem appropriate at the time, is that the congregation is tyrannized by the preacher's own preferences. This can be avoided when preaching is planned within the context of the liturgical year, with a series of texts or pericopes suggested for each Sunday. During Advent, for example, the preacher would deal with the whole matter of incarnation, prophecy, and fulfillment, culminating in the festival of Christmas. It would mean, too, that preaching over the entire year would include treatment of the whole life, ministry, suffering, death, resurrection, and ascension of Jesus and the birth of the church. The minister cannot ignore, delete, or rip out sections of the biblical proclamation simply because they do not interest him or her or because they seem arcane, or worse yet, irrelevant!

The use of the church-year lectionary forces the preacher to deal responsibly with the total expression of the Christian faith as propounded in creeds and confessions. It affirms that there are traditions and a body of belief hammered out in the past by faithful people who struggled as we do, to express in some rational fashion what Jesus Christ meant to them and how they saw this indicated in the Bible. It is a challenge to one's own faith and presuppositions. Furthermore, it shifts the weight of responsiblity for the subject matter of a sermon from our feeble shoulders and limited minds. The minister who, week in and week out, must face that harrowing question, What shall I preach next Sunday? will dry up in a few years. It will become apparent all too soon that what that minister feels or thinks becomes the content of his or her preaching. One must maintain a healthy and constant engagement between one's own deeply felt theological convictions and the total subject matter of the gospel. Certainly the sermon is one's own creation, shaped by one's own beliefs, but this is not a totally subjective, private affair or a dialogue wholly within oneself.

This concern for theological breadth leads us to an essential element in developing a theology of preaching—a thorough and continuous immersion in the Bible. Sermons are fundamentally developed upon biblical texts and take their shape and direction from them. The study of the Bible in a formal sense, therefore, is necessary for preaching. Furthermore, the ultimate shape of one's theology of preaching must express one's own understanding of the Bible's message as an essential dimension of its form. It is true of course, that the Bible is many books, dealing with a variety of themes and written in many forms, over a long period of time. It is also true that within this diversity there is a kind of unity. Barth speaks of this unity when he maintains that ultimately the Bible is not dealing with the human condition, but with God's movement toward us in Jesus Christ. Whatever one may wish to make of this statement, it does offer a way of relating or holding together the various elements in the many books of the Bible. It is my opinion that far too few seminarians have studied and meditated upon the Scriptures. They take courses in the New and Old Testaments, but they do not live with the Bible so that it becomes their life. Often they do not see how courses on Bible, theology, and preaching are interrelated as a common discipline. The blame is not to be placed upon seminarians, however, but upon seminary instruction, which tends far too much to separate and enclose the various areas of study into fields or departments. The seminary curriculum often symbolizes the unrelatedness rather than the essential interconnection of the courses.

Beyond the obvious need to develop interdisciplinary study, however, and to encourage seminarians to integrate areas of knowledge, there is the need for meditation with the Bible. The use of the "callatio" method, introduced in many seminaries by Jesuits under the influence of Loyola's *Spiritual Exercises*, is one way of developing a much-needed discipline in prayer and Bible study. In this technique, a text is read aloud to a small group, and an extended period of quiet meditation follows. Then each member of the group is invited to express his or her personal feelings about the significance of that text. No one is required to speak out, and there is no feedback from the others present. The text is read again and another opportunity is given for personal reflection. The period, which may last half an hour, ends with prayer. The purpose of this discipline, which is geared to groups but may also be used effectively by an individual, is to develop an awareness of one's own feelings about the faith one proclaims. It enables participants to form and root themselves more completely in the Christ who is proclaimed. It encourages a kind of personal authenticity—an integrity which breaks through the many facades we create. It is this authentic note, this essential honesty and dependency upon the Bible, that shines through in our preaching as our own testimony. Barth, it seems to me, is quite right in insisting again and again that preaching must begin in prayer. We all too human and struggling people will not know what or how to preach until we find our roots and are nourished by prayer and its essential guide, the Bible.

Fosdick, it will be remembered, calls us "to think the great faiths of the Gospel through in contemporary terms." The person most thoroughly acquainted with the great faiths of the gospel is most apt to be able to do this. The more one steeps oneself in this source of life, the greater freedom one feels to interpret its message in contemporary terms. One cannot translate ancient terms or find appropriate figures of speech that appeal to the modern mind unless one knows the original source of the phrases and understands their various uses. The sermon that speaks to people is one in which the faith has become newly spoken.

There is much to be said for Tillich's bold and often exciting attempts either to find new images or to infuse traditional religious language with new life. There is a tendency to believe that a religious term is an exact description of an objective reality, which can be envisioned or understood by means of that specific term, and no other. We see this belief at work in the way evangelistic preachers such as Billy Graham speak of Satan, for example. "He" is embodied and considered a person—an objective being who confronts us. Tillich conceives of the term "Satan" as a metaphor to describe our sense of being confronted by powers and principalities that overwhelm us, tempt us, divide us. The experiences are real enough, but to objectify them in terms of a person or a power that is too precise may actually soften the impact of the image, simply because it is too literally stated. Liberals seldom deal with the subject in sermons; for them, "Satan" represents the evils in society and in ourselves that make us selfish and prevent the coming of the kingdom of God. Satan, in Cleage's sermons, is quite plainly the "white" society that has dominated and controlled blacks. Satan, to paraphrase Sartre, is "other people."

I share the belief that exciting preaching in our age occurs when one is liberated from the belief that religious language must be understood as primarily, or only, biblical language. It seems to me that language is a vehicle of revelation, but is not itself revelation. As we have seen in this chapter, the texts of the Bible disclose their writers' quest for appropriate language to proclaim the faith, and the terms chosen are found in the culture of those eras.

I believe that the more we know about the Bible, the more we will feel the excitement and challenge it conveys, and the more we will desire to communicate its life-giving promises to others in the language of our times, so that they may hear and believe; because they *can* hear! We should not be afraid to risk such a creative, imaginative activity. It is not a denial of our heritage, but a continuation of the groping, meaningful task carried on by others who went before us. We are all living, I think, in "a kind of spiritual kindergarten, where bewildered infants are trying to spell God with the wrong blocks."[4] Or to shift the poet's image somewhat, each generation struggles with the task of saying what it deeply affirms but finds so hard to express.

I recite the creeds and confessions of the church during public worship, conscious that many of their metaphors create pictures that are foreign to me, or strange, or that simply are not conceivable. I feel that in participating in these past formulations of the beliefs and proclamations of faithful people, I am honoring their expression of faith. At the same time, I recognize the distance between us in time, culture, and world-view. I am grateful to the theological fathers and mothers of the church, but it does not follow that I should or can agree with all of them. What I must attempt, as a faith-filled Christian in this age, is to say what I believe to the people of this era. This is an enormous responsibility, an exhilarating burden, and a dreadful opportunity. It is what we as preachers are called to do.

NOTES

CHAPTER I: Neo-orthodoxy: Karl Barth

1. Karl Barth and Eduard Thurneysen, *Come Holy Spirit*, trans. George W. Richards (New York: Round Table Press, 1934), pp. 101-2.
2. *Ibid.*, pp. 90-91.
3. Barth, *Deliverance to the Captives*, trans. Marguerite Wiesser (New York: Harper & Brothers, 1961), pp. 35-36.
4. *Come Holy Spirit*, pp. 196-97.
5. *Deliverance to Captives*, pp. 44-45.
6. Barth, *Church Dogmatics*, trans. G. T. Thomson and Harold Knight (Edinburgh: T. & T. Clark, 1963), vol. 1, pt. 1, pp. 729-35.
7. Barth, *The Epistle to the Romans*, trans. Edwyn C. Hoskins (London: Oxford University Press, 1968), p. 8.
8. Barth, *Christmas*, trans. Berhard Citron (London: Oliver & Boyd, 1959), p. 25.
9. *Come Holy Spirit*, p. 95.
10. *Deliverance to Captives*, p. 66.
11. *Ibid.*, p. 37.
12. *Ibid.*, p. 133.
13. *Ibid.*, p. 32.
14. *Church Dogmatics*, vol. 4, pt. 1, p. 269.
15. *Deliverance to Captives*, p. 77.
16. *Come Holy Spirit*, p. 85.
17. *Deliverance to Captives*, p. 35.
18. *Church Dogmatics*, vol. 1, pt. 1, p. 255.

CHAPTER II: Existentialism: Paul Tillich

1. Paul Tillich, *The Shaking of the Foundations* (New York: Charles Scribner's Sons, 1948), pp. 93-94.
2. Tillich, *The New Being* (New York: Charles Scribner's Sons, 1955), p. 121.

3. *The Courage to Be* (New Haven: Yale University Press, 1959).

4. *New Being*, p. 41.

5. *Shaking of Foundations*, pp. 127-28.

6. Tillich, *On the Boundary* (New York: Charles Scribner's Sons, 1966).

7. *New Being*, p. 37.

8. Tillich, *Systematic Theology*, 3 vols. (1951-63; reprinted, Chicago: University of Chicago Press, 1957), vol. 2, p. 61.

9. Tillich, *The Eternal Now* (New York: Charles Scribner's Sons, 1963), p. 62.

10. *New Being*, p. 7.

11. Baldwin, *The Fire Next Time* (New York: Dial Press, 1963), p. 130.

12. *New Being*, p. 23.

13. *Shaking of Foundations*, p. 4.

14. *Ibid.*, p. 67.

15. *New Being*, p. 53.

16. *Ibid.*

17. *Eternal Now*, p.176.

18. *Ibid.*, p. 177.

19. *New Being*, p. 73.

20. *Systematic Theology*, vol. 2, p. 122.

21. *New Being*, p. 98.

22. *Ibid.*, p. 100.

CHAPTER III: Liberalism: The American School

1. Fosdick, *Adventurous Living* (New York: Harper & Brothers, 1926), p. 257.

2. James Cox, *Twentieth-Century Pulpit* (Nashville: Abingdon, 1978), p. 63.

3. Fosdick, *Modern Use of the Bible* (New York: The Macmillan Co., 1925).

4. Gilkey, *A Faith for the New Generation* (New York: The Macmillan Co., 1926), p. 37.

5. Charles M. Crowe, ed., *Great Southern Preaching* (New York: The Macmillan Co., 1926), p. 128.

6. Joseph Fort Newton, *The New Preaching* (Nashville: Cokesbury Press, 1930), pp. 73-74.

7. Newton, ed., *Best Sermons 1926* (New York: Harcourt, Brace & Co., 1926), p. 151.

8. Charles C. Morrison, ed., *The American Pulpit* (New York: The Macmillan Co., 1927), pp. 346-47, 351.

9. Fosdick, *The Living of These Days* (New York: Harper & Brothers, 1956), p. 92.

10. Newton, *New Preaching*, pp. 139, 142.

11. Macintosh, *The Problem of Religious Knowledge* (New York: Harper & Brothers, 1940), pp. 192-93.

12. Charles R. Brown, "Keeping the Faith," *Christianity and Modern Thought*, ed. Ralph H. Gabriel (New Haven: Yale University Press, 1924), p. 16.

13. Theodore G. Soares, ed., *University of Chicago Sermons* (University of Chicago Press, 1915), p. 244.

14. Roy L. Smith, *Suburban Christians* (New York: Harper & Brothers, 1933), p. 63.

15. Thomas B. Mather, ed., *Voices of the Living Prophets* (Nashville: Cokesbury Press, 1933), pp. 179-80.

16. Newton, ed., *Best Sermons 1924* (New York: Harcourt, Brace & Co., 1924), p. 189.

17. Ralph Sockman, *Suburbs of Christianity* (New York: Abingdon Press, 1924), pp. 127-29.

18. Newton, ed., *Best Sermons 1925* (New York: Harcourt, Brace & Co., 1925), pp. 226-27.

19. Gladden, *Present Day Theology* (Columbus, Ohio: McClelland & Co., 1913), pp. 137-38.

20. Newton, ed., *Best Sermons 1927* (New York: Harcourt, Brace & Co., 1927), pp. 159, 164.

21. Sockman, *The Highway of God* (New York: The Macmillan Co., 1942), pp. 217-18

22. Fosdick, *Living Under Tension* (New York: Harper & Brothers, 1942), p. 49.

23. Smith, *Suburban Christians*, p. 15.

24. Coffin, *God's Turn* (New York: Harper & Brothers, 1934), p. 55.

25. Niebuhr, *Leaves from the Notebooks of a Tamed Cynic* (New York: World Publishing Co., Meridian Books, 1960), p. 218.

CHAPTER IV: Fundamentalism: The Evangelists

1. "Evangelistic" refers to the general intention or goal of such sermons. "Fundamentalism" refers to the doctrinal positions of preachers, who may differ somewhat among themselves theologically, but who nevertheless share a common concern to evangelize.

2. Billy (William F.) Graham, *The Challenge* (Garden City, N.Y.: Doubleday & Co., 1969), p. 69.

3. *Ibid.*, p. 78.

4. John R. Bisagno, *The Power of Positive Preaching to the Saved* (Nashville: Broadman Press, 1971), p. 19.

5. Hyman J. Appelman, ed., *Great Gospel Sermons* (New York: Fleming H. Revell, 1949), vol. 2, pp. 11-12.

6. V. P. Black, *We Persuade Men*, 20th Century Sermons, J. D. Thomas, ed. (Abilene, Tex.: Biblical Research Press, 1969), vol. 2, p. 31.

7. Graham, *Challenge*, p. 71.

8. Black, *We Persuade Men*, vol. 2, p. 103.

9. John R. Bisagno, *The Power of Positive Preaching to the Lost* (Nashville: Broadman Press, 1972), p. 69.

10. "Genuine Christianity," Appelman, *Great Gospel Sermons*, vol. 2, p. 32.

11. Harold J. Ockenga, "The Man Who Lived for the World Only," Appleman, *Great Gospel Sermons*, p. 170.

12. Graham, *Challenge*, p. 81.

13. *Ibid.*, p. 69.

14. Bisagno, *Positive Preaching to Lost*, p. 70.
15. James E. Kilgore, *Billy Graham the Preacher* (New York: Exposition Press, 1969), chap. 6.
16. Graham, *Challenge*, p. 77.
17. *Ibid.*, p. 84.

CHAPTER V: Black Liberationism: Albert B. Cleage, Jr.

1. For the most recent and most helpful material intersecting liberation theology and preaching, see Justo and Catherine Gonzales' *Liberation Preaching: The Pulpit and the Oppressed* (Nashville: Abingdon, 1980).
2. Albert B. Cleage, Jr., *The Black Messiah* (New York: Sheed & Ward, 1968), p. 201.
3. Robert W. Duke, "Black Theology and the Experience of Blackness," *The Journal of Religious Thought*, vol. 29 (Spring/Summer 1972), p. 28.
4. Cleage, *Black Messiah*, p. 204.
5. *Ibid.*, p. 98.
6. *Ibid.*, p. 109.
7. *Ibid.*, p. 209.
8. *Ibid.*, p. 97.
9. Before one indulges in a hasty critique of Cleage, one should read *Black Rage* by William H. Grier and Price M. Cobbs (New York: Basic Books, 1968), together with its companion volume by the same authors, *The Jesus Bag* (New York: McGraw-Hill Book Co., 1971).
10. Cleage, *Black Messiah*, p. 111.
11. *Ibid.*, p. 52.
12. *Ibid.*
13. *Ibid.*, p. 41.
14. *Ibid.*, p. 92.
15. *Ibid.*, p. 61.
16. *Ibid.*, p. 62.
17. *Ibid.*, p. 74.
18. *Ibid.*, p. 81.
19. *Ibid.*, p. 82, 84.
20. *Ibid.*, p. 93.
21. Johnson, *God's Trombones* (New York: Viking Press, 1950).
22. Cone, *Black Theology and Black Power* (New York: Seabury Press, 1969). See chap. 6 in particular.

CHAPTER VI: Developing a Theology to Preach

1. S.F.G. Brandon, *The Trial of Jesus* (London: Granada Publishing, Ltd., Paladin Books, 1971). See also by the same author, *Jesus and the Zealots* (Manchester, Eng.: Manchester University Press, 1967).
2. Ernst Käsemann, *New Testament Questions Today*, trans. W. J. Montague (London: SCM Press, 1969), p. 8.

3. Kornelius H. Miskotte, *When the Gods are Silent*, trans. John W. Doberstein (New York: Harper & Row, 1967), p. 150.
4. Edwin Arlington Robinson, *Modern American and Modern British Poetry*, ed. Louis Untermeyer (New York: Harcourt, Brace & Co., 1942), p. 139.

FOR FURTHER READING

CHAPTER I: Neo-orthodoxy: Karl Barth

Barth, Karl. *Preaching Through the Christian Year: A Selection of Exegetical Passages from the Church Dogmatics.* Translated by G. W. Bromiley and T. F. Torrance. Edited by John McTavish and Harold Wells. Grand Rapids: Eerdmans Publishing Co., 1978.
———. *The Word of God and the Word of Man.* Translated by Douglas Horton. New York: Harper Torchbooks, 1957.
Come, Arnold B. *An Introduction to Barth's "Dogmatics" for Preachers.* Philadelphia: Westminster Press, 1963.
Ritschl, Dietrich. *A Theology of Proclamation.* Richmond: John Knox Press, 1960.

CHAPTER II: Existentialism: Paul Tillich

Hopper, David. *Tillich: A Theological Portrait.* Philadelphia: J. B. Lippincott Co., 1968.
Lyons, James R., ed. *The Intellectual Legacy of Paul Tillich.* Detroit: Wayne State University Press, 1969.
Tavard, George H. *Paul Tillich and the Christian Message.* New York: Charles Scribner's Sons, 1962.
Tillich, Paul. *On the Boundary.* New York: Charles Scribner's Sons, 1966.
———. *The Protestant Era.* Translated by James Luther Adams. Chicago: The University of Chicago Press, 1953.

CHAPTER III: Liberalism: The American School

Cauthen, Kenneth. *The Impact of American Religious Liberalism.* New York: Harper & Row, 1962.
Cobb, John B. *Liberal Christianity at the Crossroads.* Philadelphia: Westminster Press, 1973.
Fosdick, Harry E. *A Guide to Understanding the Bible: The Development of Ideas Within the Old and New Testaments.* New York: Harper & Brothers, 1938.
———. *The Living of These Days.* New York: Harper & Brothers, 1956.

Van Dusen, Henry P. *The Vindication of Liberal Theology: A Tract for the Times*. New York: Charles Scribner's Sons, 1963.

CHAPTER IV: Fundamentalism: The Evangelists

Barr, James. *Fundamentalism*. Philadelphia: Westminster Press, 1978.
Henry, Carl F. H., ed. *Christian Faith and Modern Theology*. 2 vols. New York: Channel Press, 1964.
Pollock, John. *Billy Graham: Evangelist to the World*. New York: Harper & Row, 1979.
Settel, T. S., ed. *The Faith of Billy Graham*. Anderson, S.C.: Droke House, 1968.

CHAPTER V: Black Liberationism: Albert B. Cleage, Jr.

Bruce, Calvin E. and Jones, William R., eds. *Black Theology II: Essays on the Formation and Outreach of Contemporary Black Theology*. Lewisburg, Pa.: Bucknell University Press, 1978.
Cleage, Albert B., Jr. *Black Christian Nationalism*. New York: William Morrow & Co., 1972.
Gardiner, James J. and Roberts, Deotis, eds. *Quest for a Black Theology*. Philadelphia: United Church Press, 1971.
Jones, Major J. *Black Awareness*. Nashville: Abingdon Press, 1971.
Mitchell, Henry H. *Black Preaching*. Philadelphia: J.B. Lippincott Co., 1970.
Roberts, Deotis. A *Black Theology*. Philadelphia: Westminster Press, 1974.
Wilmore, Gayraud S. and Cone, James H., eds. *Black Theology: A Documentary History, 1966–1979*. Maryknoll, N.Y.: Orbis Books, 1979.

CHAPTER VI: Developing a Theology to Preach

Gilkey, Langdon. *Naming the Whirlwind: The Renewal of God Language*. New York: Bobbs-Merrill, 1969.
Keck, Leander E. *The Bible in the Pulpit: The Renewal of Biblical Preaching*. Nashville: Abingdon, 1978.
Thielicke, Helmut. *The Trouble with the Church*. Translated and edited by John W. Doberstein. New York: Harper & Row, 1965.

INDEX OF SUBJECTS

INDEX OF BIBLICAL REFERENCES